The Future of the Jews

By the same author

The Inequality of States (1967)

The Making of British Foreign Policy (1968)

The Survival of Small States: Studies in Small Power/Great Power Conflict (1971)

The Origins of Zionism (1975)

Zionism: The Formative Years (1982)

Zionism: The Crucial Phase (1987)

The Future of the Jews

DAVID VITAL

HARVARD UNIVERSITY PRESS
Cambridge, Massachusetts, and London, England   1990

This book is printed on acid-free paper, and its binding
materials have been chosen for strength and durability.

Library of Congress Cataloging-in-Publication Data

Vital, David.
  The future of the Jews / David Vital.
    p.   cm.
  ISBN 0–674–33925–8
  1. Israel and the Diaspora.
2. Jews—United States—Attitudes toward Israel.
I. Title.
DS132.V58   1990
973′.04924—dc20   90–4152
                                         CIP

For my children,
Tamar, Adam, and Ruthie

Preface

This book owes its existence to a generous invitation that enabled me to teach at an American university, while continuing to hold a regular appointment at my home university at Tel Aviv. I was thus in a position to see aspects of American—but most especially Jewish-American—life somewhat more closely and continuously than had been the case in the past. More particularly, owing to the timing (1988–89), I found myself witness to a particularly steep rise in the long-standing but hitherto somewhat muted tension between large sections of the Jewish-American public and the state and people—and, of course, the government—of Israel.

The great outpouring of ostensibly frank speaking, the repeated flashes of intense irritation, the rising mutual alienation (enough of it being articulated to suggest that much was suppressed)—to all of which ever wider circles of the general public were exposed—have been distressing to observe and register. But while they were especially painful to one who has spent a good part of his academic life investigating the rise of the very movement—the Zionist movement—which tends to be charged with the historical (if ironic) responsibility for the present disarray in Jewry, these manifestations of resentment and frustration were not unexpected. And if the debate is now very heated, and the disarray in which the Jews *qua* Jews now generally find themselves is now fully manifest, one cannot say that there is anything really new about the intemperance of expression, or the looseness of argument, or the actual issues and the roots of the trouble—or, of course, the trouble itself. These are no more than the spin-off effects of the ever-accelerating, still unfinished revolution in Jewish life that has been in progress since the movement's foundation a century ago.

What is alarming and especially depressing to note are the superficial, ill-informed, and often positively false terms in which the issues relevant to the present great debate in Jewry have tended, by and large, to be put before the public. And what is really new, although, on the contrary, encouraging, is what seems to me to be the beginning of something like a disposition in the Diaspora to look at the matter and the dilemmas of contemporary Jewry with a sharper eye than has tended to be in evidence heretofore; and, too, most difficult of all, perhaps, finally to screw up enough courage to call a spade a spade.

I do not think that it can yet be said that clear-sightedness, a calm spirit, and real and consistent intellectual honesty are actually breaking out all over. Obfuscation, hidden agenda, double-talk, and, commonest of all, double-think are still very much the order of the day. (I have tried to explore some of the reasons for this; much remains wholly beyond my comprehension.) Nevertheless, the heat of the debate and the power of the forces that are pulling the Jewish people apart do appear to be stripping away some of the social and psychological obstacles to plain speaking and frank debate—many of which, for well understood reasons, are of very ancient lineage in the public life of the Jews.

This is a welcome development. For my part, at any rate (as will be evident from what follows), I am entirely in favor of plain speaking. I do most sincerely believe that when really serious and important questions are finally tackled, plain speaking has got to be the first order of the day.

Contents

The Future of the Jews

ONE

The Plunge into Modernity

No more than two centuries ago, the notion that great numbers of Jews would *want* to be admitted to civil society was fully as daring, and as revolutionary in its consequences, as the parallel notion that it might well be right and proper to admit them. Within Jewry it was daring because it entailed the sharpest possible break with precedent among a people for whom precedent had long since become the very armature of their collective existence. It was revolutionary—as radical reformers were no slower to see than the orthodox who opposed them—because, by the time such questions had begun to surface in the public consciousness to any effect, "civil society" in Europe had commonly come to mean national society. No matter what gloss you tried to put on such change, to enter French, German, English, Italian, or any other society was, at the very least, heavily to discount the national content of the life of the Jews themselves and virtually to dissolve the national component of that great complex (not to say tangle) of history, high culture, belief, and social and ritual practice we call Judaism. No wonder the great precipitants of change in the aims and behavior of countless individuals, but above all change in the degree of receptivity of Jews to new ideas, *whence* their new mood, aims, and social and political behavior, were released by events wholly external to Jewry. These, so the textbooks tell us, were the European Enlightenment, capped in turn by the convulsion of the French Revolution and the Napoleonic wars that followed it. For once the textbooks are right.

The importance of the events of 1789 so far as the Jews were concerned was, of course, that for the first time since the establishment of Christianity as the preponderant religion in Europe they were offered—or seemed to be offered—equality of status with all other citizens. But note: *citizens.* The Jews, that is to say, were offered a form of membership in the larger community that we now regard as normal but at the time was startlingly new. It was an offer of citizenship with many or all of the advantages that citizenship implied, and still implies: equality before the law, participation in the political process, access to public office, but also the regular obligations of military duty and fiscal contribution. Strictly speaking, the offer was not made immediately; and when it was made, it was made with certain reservations. Even when all the reservations attached to it had finally been removed and it was passed into legislation, it was still—and is still—an open question whether French Jews, to take the prime example, were ever to find themselves on an entirely equal social basis with their new compatriots. Nevertheless, the decisive facts were that the *principle* of universal legal and political equality had been raised in the new French Republic; and that, having been raised, it was not long before the principle was authoritatively proclaimed and legislated. Neither in France nor anywhere else had it ever been raised and discussed in such terms before. Still less had it

2

been proclaimed. And, accordingly, never before had a Jewish community been faced with the need to consider what civil liberty and legal equality might really mean for it. Never before had the question of how such a community's members should work out the necessary readjustment in their own private and collective lives—an adjustment that could not fail to be of a profoundly revolutionary nature in itself—been posed with such precision and such urgency.

It is worth stressing that the offer of citizenship to the Jews of France came in the shape of a reform based on abstract principles and as a matter of universal propriety and justice. Its terms, that is to say, were general. From the standpoint of the revolutionaries in Paris, the specific question of the largish community of Jews in Alsace and the very much smaller communities elsewhere in France merited treatment only as part of what purported to be an entirely new conception of how society *as a whole* should be organized and governed. As seen by its proponents, the Emancipation was therefore in no sense a matter of rendering the Jews justice and recompense long denied them. If anything, the contrary was true. Hostility to them was alive and strong, notably in Alsace, whence it was communicated very effectively and speedily to Paris. It was the Jews as a specific social category who were seen as owing a debt to society—a debt which those who favored the Emancipation believed the Jews themselves would now begin to comprehend and not only have an opportunity to pay, but be more than willing to pay. Those who argued on their behalf did not deny the Jews' alleged faults and misbehavior. Rather they sought excuses for them; and they advanced as their central claim that a new deal for the Jews was precisely what was

3

needed to make it possible for a newly benevolent society to bring this very unsatisfactory (but neither hopeless nor wholly wicked) people up to scratch.

In these circumstances, it cannot surprise us that the initial response of many of the Jews concerned to the demands made *of* them, no less than to those made *on their behalf*, was at least as embarrassed and anxious as it was hopeful and here and there even enthusiastic. And the effect was to put those who would now be the most "advanced" of European Jews on the defensive in their relations with non-Jews in a way that was new and ominous and fated in time to become exceedingly familiar. Such was certainly the case in the short term in France, where the prospect of definitive emancipation was as good as immediate, but equally in the long term elsewhere in Europe, even where the prospect of emancipation was still remote and where the initial response to developments in France can best be characterized as watchful.

But the real catch to the offer of emancipation lay in the fact that virtually all French revolutionaries—moderates no less than radicals, Dantonists no less than Robespierrists, Christians as well as deists or pantheists or atheists—believed that equality of status in the modern state they wished to establish was necessarily bound up with the elimination of all such classes or corporations as were intermediate, and mediating, between the State and the citizen. All social classes and categories had to go—however they were defined, whatever their specific nature, regardless of their purpose, whether or not they were endowed with special rights, prerogatives, status, or duties. This applied to the aristocracy, of course. It applied to old-style guilds and corporations where these retained ancient privileges in the manner that we would now call medieval. It applied to the established Roman Catholic Church. It applied equally to non-Catholic religious groups and sects, notably the Protestant. Finally and necessarily, it applied to all alien national or ethnic groups in the sense that it would now be for their members to decide whether they were to become Frenchmen, or were to remain foreigners—still tolerated, quite possibly, but wholly outside the circle of recognized citizenship and political participation.

The Jews, taken together, were evidently a "church." They were evidently a national group as well. Having their own long-standing and long-accepted system of internal jurisdiction, they were, quite as evidently, a "corporation" in very much that medieval form and sense which was now to be swept away. With respect to these people, accordingly, there was more than one set of questions to be asked and debated; and there was more than one count on which they were fated—as a collectivity—to be condemned. Were the Jews Frenchmen or were they aliens? Could they conceivably become Frenchmen if, as seemed evident, they were not? And if so, on what terms? But secondly, what did the Jews themselves really intend? Did they want to be Frenchmen? Did they want to be citizens? All of which was to imply, as even the most enthusiastic of the proponents of Jewish emancipation recognized at the time, that there would have to be an answer to a larger question: Were the Jews really prepared, as part of the promised release from their long-standing disabilities, to give up what was seen by all to be their ancient propensity to isolation, to organization in self-contained communities, to the settlement of their affairs and disputes among themselves and by themselves, and to marriage exclusively within the community and the faith?

In brief, the question now posed by the very logic of the

5

Emancipation was that of the Jews' continued identity as a distinct people. It could not have been posed with greater clarity. It is the central question facing Jewry to this day. The fundamental division of opinion, outlook, and perceived interests within contemporary Jewry is precisely between those who are prepared to answer the question as clearly as it has been posed these past two hundred years and those who are not.

It may be worth recalling that what loomed behind this great issue was no less than that which lay at the very foundation of the political and social outlook of the French revolutionaries themselves: the idea of the Nation. The Nation, for the new leaders of France, was as much a philosophical as a practical political idea. In the view they propagated, it was the sovereign, unitary <u>Nation</u> that would now replace the King under God as the fundamental social and political entity in terms of which the highest public good might be determined and the source of all legitimate authority derived. It followed that there could be no room any more for distinct and separate peoples with distinct and separate rules of behavior— not within a single state, that is, least of all within their own French Republic. There could certainly be no room for closed groups which seemed positively to rejoice in being insulated socially, to some extent economically too, perhaps even politically, but certainly mentally and culturally, from the rest of the population. It was barely conceivable that such groups be tolerated as strangers. It was wholly inconceivable that they be admitted to full membership in society and regular citizenship. For so far as the structure and processes of government were concerned, what the revolutionaries wanted most urgently was not so much equality of official treatment of

the individual as, in the final analysis, a high degree of uni-
formity within the citizenry as well. No longer was France to
be an untidy complex of estates, guilds, classes, and corporations, all loosely supervised from above, none totally devoid of
autonomy and the capacity to go its own way. There was now
to be a strictly defined, sovereign, central, secular authority of
virtually untrammeled power, fit to represent all and to govern
all without encountering entrenched or inalienable or special
and peculiar prerogatives of any kind. But in such a system,
could room be found for Jewry as traditionally constituted?
Manifestly, the answer was no.

The power and simplicity of this philosophy were reflected
in the casual—if possibly unthinking—brutality of treatment
meted out to the Jews in the course of the revolutionary government's initial attempts to deal with them. Such was the case
in Alsace, notably, and to some extent in Lorraine, for there
the Jews were generally thought to present a problem war-
ranting especially firm action. This was partly by reason of
their numbers—small in absolute terms, but great enough to
ensure visibility—but also because of the involvement of a
substantial number of local Jews in the always and inevitably
bitter, not to say nasty and dangerous, business of extending
financial credit. It was credit against interest, naturally enough,
exposing the Jews to the charge thought to be peculiarly applicable to them: usury.

This was an ancient charge against them with roots in
medieval Christianity's insistent repression and humiliation of
the Jews, forcing them out of virtually all socially acceptable
occupations and damning and despising them for taking up
whatever was left: peddling, dealing in second-hand cloth-

7

ing, pawnbroking, and making straightforward money loans against interest. Its continuing force goes part of the way, although only part of the way, to explain the special hostility towards them evinced by the new rulers of France. And it is interesting to note other very telling ways in which the strict atheism—or at best, deism—of the republicans continued to be nourished by old-style, essentially Christian dislikes and prejudices, not to say ignorance.

As it happened, many Jews did their level best to accommodate themselves to the new regime. Torah scrolls were put away. Synagogues were closed. Ritual candelabra were handed over to municipal authorities. Beards were shaved off. Dress was revised. And much of this was voluntary. But not all; and the process of adjustment and change was neither speedy nor complete enough to satisfy all the new administrators. Peremptory demands to hasten and intensify the process were not infrequent—as when on 23 Brumaire of the Year Two of the new revolutionary calender (13 November 1793) the authorities in Nancy called on the "republicans and philosophers of the former Jewish religion" to hand over "their mystical charters as well as . . . all objects of gold or silver, furniture, ornaments, [and other artifacts and] emblems serving a ritual purpose."[1] Nor could such demands be ignored. The harshness and inflexibility of the approach with which the newly emancipated Jews of France had often to contend is conveyed by the terms in which charges of religiosity were leveled against the Jews of Strasbourg on the first of Frimaire (21 November) of the same year. Specifically, it was argued against them, they had unconscionably continued to observe the Sabbath, to engage in the ritual slaughter of animals, to circumcise their infant sons, and to wear distinctive clothing.

It is the inhumane law amongst these people [the district procurator asserted] that the newborn male infant is to be bloodily operated upon as if nature herself were imperfect. They wear long beards with ostentation and to mimic the patriarchs whose virtues they themselves have failed to inherit. They employ a language of which they are ignorant and which has long since fallen into disuse. In consequence, I call upon the provisional commission that it forbid them such practices and arrange for an autodafé [*sic*] to Truth of all Hebrew books and most especially of the Talmud, the author of which was so rascally as to permit them to make usurious loans to men who are not of their faith.[2]

Still, in the early, dangerous, and tumultuous years of revolutionary and republican France the matter of the Jews was hardly one to which great and consistent attention was paid. The Jews represented only one of a vast number of problems and anomalies which needed to be tidied up. Their affairs were given something like serious attention only after the rise of Napoleon, as a result of his remarkable effort to establish not only a new system of law but also, and in some ways more especially, a fresh social and political order for all of France—an effort that has done much to shape France to this day. But if this new order was more systematic, it was nonetheless imbued with much the same spirit.

In the minds of the leaders of the new Empire, there were, broadly speaking, three difficulties about the Jews. One was administrative. Once the revolutionary and ideology-intensive approach to government and politics had been at least partly replaced—at any rate modified—by Napoleonic pragmatism and opportunism, relations with the Roman Catholic Church, and with the French Reformed (or Protestant) Church too, could be, and in short order were, put on an orderly basis. That left only the Jews; and the new, tidily-minded Napoleonic administrators recognized that, sooner or later, they would have to deal with them too. Indeed, they were to be reminded afresh of the need as from time to time disputes within the Jewish community, no longer so inhibited against calling for external intervention in its internal affairs as in the past, boiled over into the country at large and came before the imperial authorities. In one case which has been recorded, the government found, reluctantly, that it had to contend with the rabbi and the elders of an Alsatian community pitted against a man whom they had expelled from their midst. When he and his family found themselves denied the traditional services of *shohet*[3] and *mikve*[4] on which they felt entitled to rely, they proceeded to lodge an appeal against their expulsion with the civil authorities. It was precisely because such recourse to extra-communal authority ran wholly against the grain of traditional Jewish practice and had always been rare that it landed the authorities with an issue of which they had no experience, let alone machinery and precedents to rely upon. Whom, in such a case, was the departmental prefect to support? The private citizen with a seemingly legitimate grievance? Or the established communal leaders through whom, evidently, this particular community could be most efficiently controlled?

There was a second difficulty. The makers and the legatees of the French Revolution were, after all, men of the Enlightenment, which amounts to saying that their approach to the needs and problems of society was fundamentally ahistorical. Their minds were set on the universal, as opposed to the particular. They tended very largely to see things and to define issues so far as possible in abstract terms—in terms, as we would now say, of "models." Above all, *reason* had to be the great determinant of social questions, so far as they were concerned: not revelation, or faith, or grace, or—least of all—ancient authority. It followed, in their view, that if the world was to be built anew—a better, cleaner, neater, above all more rational world, a world from first principles—then much of the past and its incongruities had to be sloughed off. But could this be a world in which the Jews too—always, to many European minds, the most peculiar social category of all—would find a place for themselves? More precisely, was this a world in which the men of the Enlightenment themselves and in particular could be expected to help find a place for them? Their difficulty in coming to terms with the problem owed much to the circumstance that to the irritation and offense engendered in them by the plain fact of the Jews' particularity and eccentricity there was added an endemic dislike (not to say detestation) of the Jews which stemmed, on the one hand, as already suggested, from the old Christian legacy to which even these new men were in one way or another, consciously or otherwise, still heirs; and, equally and paradoxically, on the other hand, from their tendency, as sons of the Enlightenment, to see Christianity itself—to which their underlying hostility still ran deep—as a faith and a system derived in many central respects from Jewish origins.

Writing a decade or so before the French Revolution, Edward Gibbon, very much a man of the same European Enlightenment of which the Paris Declaration of the Rights of Man and Citizen of 1789 was such notable fruit, had this to say of the Jews: "A single people refused to join in the common intercourse of mankind. . . . The sullen obstinacy with which they maintained their peculiar rites and unsocial manners

11

seemed to mark them out as a distinct species of men, who boldly professed, or who faintly disguised, their implacable hatred to the rest of human kind."[5] As a witty attempt to sum up the matter of the Jews, this passage is characteristic of Gibbon. As a fine combination of impatience, ignorance, huge intellectual and cultural arrogance, but some skewed insight too, it is hardly less characteristic of many of the men of Gibbon's own class and generation and of the generation that followed, in their approach to both the Jews of antiquity and to those of their own times.

Nevertheless, while the men of the Enlightenment were irritated by, and hostile *a priori* to, Jewish particularism, their policy towards the Jews *in practice* tended to be mitigated by the mercantilist principles to which, by and large, they were wedded. Believing that increase of population led normally to an increase of wealth, and that this was as much, if not more the case where commerce and industry, as opposed to agriculture, were concerned, they were reluctant to deal with the Jews in the drastic and peremptory manner of their medieval forebears, namely by expulsion or worse. If the Jews contributed to commerce and industry, they reasoned, it was expedient to keep them. Always *provided* they so contributed, however. Hence the distinction developed during the eighteenth century, but maintained and, if anything, sharpened in the century that followed virtually throughout Europe, between Jews who were "useful" and Jews who were not. Hence too a situation in which for those rulers who found themselves with Jewish communities to govern and to integrate in one way or another with other subjects within their modernized states, a certain contradiction arose between their political purposes and their economic ones. Of course, whereT the intellectual and politico-theoretical baggage of the Enlightenment had never been taken over in more than a limited and sparing way—as was the case in eighteenth- and nineteenth-century England—the problem presented by a Jewish presence in civil society was not thought to be so significant or serious as to demand drastic and systematic treatment in any case. There the relevant questions could be dealt with as they arose— or, as often as not, set aside. Equally, as the impact of the Enlightenment began to wear off in the course of the nineteenth century, notably in Germany, there the appeal of a reversion to ancient and vastly more brutal forms of dealing with the Jews gained strength—with eventual consequences for the Jews which are too familiar to need elaboration. But in fact, long before the final death-dealing campaign in the twentieth century, there can be seen one of the immediate and serious effects on the Jews of their rulers' working distinction between those who were useful and worth retaining, and even encouraging and certainly exploiting, and those who were not useful and were therefore "superfluous." I have in mind the strong tendency in these circumstances, for the prosperous members of Jewry, by definition the "useful" ones, to grow ever more prosperous, and for the indigent, therefore the "useless" and "superfluous" ones, to grow ever more indigent. As time went on, an ever sharper line could thus be drawn between the privileged and the underprivileged in Jewry— with, as one might expect, the privileged increasingly being those who called the tune for all.

With all this confronting them, it is hardly surprising that the response of most Jews to the root-and-branch reforming

13

spirit in which their political masters, notably in France, but in the course of time in most of continental Europe, now approached their affairs was profoundly ambivalent and apprehensive. Developments in France did nothing to assuage the apprehension.

Napoleon's basic decree on the matter of the Jews (30 May 1806) started off with an exceedingly sharp, but essentially traditional—one might say, *pre*revolutionary—denunciation of "certain Jews, whose sole occupation is that of usury." They were to be condemned, in the words of the decree, for having, by the most "immoderate" insistence on rates of interest, reduced a great many French peasants to a "condition of great distress." It was thus plainly incumbent upon the Emperor to come to the aid of those of his subjects whose circumstances had been so dreadfully reduced as a consequence of what he termed the Jews' "unjust avidity."

At the same time, it was equally urgent to go to what the government saw as the root of the matter. It was necessary, so it was proclaimed, to seek to revive active "sentiments of civic morality" in the Jews themselves. "Unfortunately," such sentiments "had slackened [*amortis*] among far too many of them as a consequence of the condition of abasement and humiliation in which they had long languished." This was a condition which he, Napoleon, was not prepared to tolerate. Accordingly, with all these considerations and purposes in mind, there would now be convoked an Assembly of Jewish Notables whose duty it would be to consider the relevant issues systematically and make specific proposals; the latter would concern methods by which the condition of their people might be corrected, ways in which they might be admitted into civil society after all,[6]

14

and means for achieving what had come to be thought of in much of polite European society by this time as the much needed "civic improvement of the Jews."

Two months later, in July 1806, a lay Assembly of Jewish notables—community leaders we would call them today, except that they were chosen by the government, not by the communities themselves—duly convened in Paris. Its work completed and the results digested by all concerned, it was followed in turn, as planned, by that famous quasi-ecclesiastical "Sanhedrin," convened in Paris in February of the following year. The function of the Sanhedrin was to provide a form of *rabbinical* sanction for the notables' formal recommendations.

But "recommendations" is hardly an appropriate term in this connection. Neither the Assembly nor the Sanhedrin was a true deliberative body. What had happened in practice was that Napoleon's commissioners presented the Jewish notables with a series of precise questions to which they were instructed to formulate their answers. These answers, taken together, were to serve them in turn, as all concerned understood perfectly well, as the basis for a lasting definition of the position of the Jews in respect of some of the great questions evoked by the Emancipation and still hanging fire. Needless to say, it was the questions as formulated and posed by the governmental commissioners that defined the issues and set the narrow framework for such discussion as took place and, of course, the terms in which first the notables, then the rabbis, were obliged to respond and make their case.

Here we come to the heart of the matter. Some of the questions put to the notables of French Jewry were no more than technical and informative. Was a Jew permitted to take more

15

than one wife? Did the Jewish religion sanction divorce? What precisely was the nature of rabbinical authority? These were easily dealt with. In contrast, the main thrust of the questionnaire to which the members of the Assembly and, later, the participants in the Sanhedrin were required to address themselves was embodied in a much more difficult set of questions. These had to do in one way or another with the terms in which the Jews proposed to see themselves as actual or future citizens of France, in fact as members of the French nation. Was it permissible, Napoleon's commissioners asked them, for Jews to intermarry with Christians? Were Frenchmen, in Jewish eyes, brethren, or were they strangers? Did a Jew born in France and treated as a citizen actually consider France his own country, one that he was bound to defend and whose laws he was bound to obey? Did Jewish law distinguish between usurious loans to Jews, presumably forbidden, and usurious loans to others, presumably permitted?

These were not questions that could be so easily answered, not without embarrassment, at any rate, or, possibly, without penalty. Still, the delegates did their best. On the two tricky questions about marriage outside the faith and usury—the latter meaning, in plain language, the extension of credit to non-Jews against interest—they were, of course, in difficulty. Alas, Jewish law being clear enough on both counts, they could only prevaricate. But in the end it was their response to the questions bearing directly on their loyalty and patriotic sentiment that was most revealing and remains of greatest and most lasting consequence. It conveyed (and still conveys) not only their own uncertainty and their extreme anxiety to please, but the essence of the very real dilemma in which they now found themselves. They declared, as firmly as they knew how, that France *was* their country and that the Jews of France *were* French patriots.

> Men who have adopted a country [they told Napoleon's commissioners], who have resided in it these many generations— who, even under the restraint of particular laws which abridged their civil rights, were so attached to it that they preferred being debarred from the advantages common to all other citizens rather than leave it—cannot but consider themselves Frenchmen in France; and they consider as equally sacred and honourable the bounden duty of defending their country . . . Love of country [they went on to say] is in the heart of Jews a sentiment so natural, so powerful, and so consonant with their religious opinions, that a French Jew considers himself in England, as among strangers, although he may be among Jews; and the case is the same with English Jews in France. To such a pitch is this sentiment carried among them, that during the last war, French Jews were fighting desperately against other Jews, the subjects of countries then at war with France.[7]

This can hardly fail to strike modern ears as a less than fully candid and dignified, let alone courageous, reply. But it would be well to remember that these were somewhat frightened, anxious, and overawed people. More decisively, perhaps, they had no precedent for dealing with the issue with which Napoleon's commissioners had confronted them. No ruler or state had ever put such questions to any analogous group of Jewish leaders—not least because there was no precedent for such a ruler as Napoleon or such a state as postrevolutionary France. They were not being asked, let alone required, as Jews had so often been asked or required in the past, to apostatize as the price of admittance to civil society. What they were being asked to clarify was less a religious than a political and cultural issue,

17

which, briefly put, was of two parts. Were both their understanding of the meaning of Jewish nationhood (or peoplehood) and their approach to it in practice truly *compatible* with effective membership in the French nation? If not, were they prepared to *modify* the former to suit the terms and needs of the latter? That was what the commissioners were driving at and most wanted to know. Now they had their answers. Whatever doubts they may have held privately—and doubts about and hostility to the Jews were much in evidence throughout these transactions—Napoleon and his ministers resolved to accept the declaration of loyalty offered them. In effect, they pronounced it satisfactory.

The immediate upshot for French Jewry was less clear-cut than the notables and rabbis seem to have anticipated, however. As a *community*, French Jewry was now to be conceived of and treated as a purely religious denomination that would be incorporated, in due course, into a typically Napoleonic framework not unlike that which had been established for the governance of other religious bodies. It would be reincorporated into—or better still, under—a system of *consistoires* which, significantly for what it tells us about modern France no less than about French Jewry, has survived, with some changes, down to the present day. But as individuals and as a *social* class, the Jews were not to enjoy fully equal treatment, even in principle, quite as rapidly as they had hoped. A generation would pass before strict legal equality was finally accorded them; and social equality, for which some now began increasingly to pine, would elude them much longer. Still, the steps taken in these early years were intensely dramatic and the entire proceedings were more effectively revolutionary than either party to the transaction seems to have realized at the time.

18

For plainly, it was not only the questions put to the Jewish notables that were without precedent. It was the answer— their claim to membership in the French nation on the basis of a *primary* loyalty to it—that was equally revolutionary. Giving it, they did much to precipitate the revolution that was to follow in all of Jewry, all of European Jewry at any rate, which was nothing less than the transformation of a hitherto discrete nation into something a great deal more complex, less coherent, and less well defined. Some would say: indefinable. Some would say: protean. Some would say: unreal.

But there was (and is) more. For it cannot be stressed too strongly that the formal emancipation of French Jewry had not come to them as a function of their neighbors' fellow-feeling or of an intrinsically and independently generous impulse from within the *classe politique* of early Republican and Napoleonic France. Nor had it been won by the Jews for themselves and by themselves. It had certainly been asked for; but the plea had not been followed up by any sort of pressure. There had been no *autonomous* application by the Jews themselves of such political and economic influence as they may have possessed in pursuance of their own stated and collective interest. No such move had been contemplated. No such move was practicable. Jews had no power or influence to speak of in late eighteenth- and early nineteenth-century France. Nor did they possess the necessary structure of internal authority, informed by the requisite degree of self-confidence, to undertake so radical a departure from the ancient Jewish tradition of quietism that was still their primary guide. In sum, the Emancipation, when it came, was a gift—awarded them (along with permission to apply for membership in society-at-large), as a function of the philosophical and political ideas on which the French revolutionary state had been founded. It had everything to do with changes in society in general and with principles that were now beginning to be thought of as universally applicable. It had very little to do with the specific condition or needs or history of the Jews themselves. Thus in France. Thus (by a different route) in Holland. Thus in a limited way and at a slower pace in Great Britain. Elsewhere in Europe, however, for all that France presented the model—and no doubt, to some extent, because the model was French—matters would proceed a lot less smoothly, or not at all.

As you traveled from the northwest corner of Europe, from west to east and from north to south, the reluctance of governments and societies to follow the French example and found the body politic on universal principles of any kind—but on those proclaimed in Paris in 1789 in particular—was ever greater. As time passed and as the French revolutionary tide (especially as embodied in the reforms imposed outside France by the Napoleonic armies) receded, so steps taken towards the emancipation of the Jews according to the French model were largely rescinded. In Rome, under the reinstated Pope Pius VII, the gates of the city's notorious ghetto were shut upon its Jewish community once more. In Frankfurt, site of an equally notorious (not to say infamous) ghetto, a concerted effort to restore the *status quo ante* was made, with a large, although not lasting, degree of success. In other German states and cities, notably in the Hansa towns of Bremen and Lübeck, Jews' right of residence was once again cut down and fresh expulsions were instituted. The hand of the Austrian government was equally heavy. In much of central Europe at least another generation, in some cases two, would pass before the promise of 1789 would be more or less fulfilled. And why "more or less"? Because everywhere, the notion of a clean sweep, of a thoroughgoing emancipation and an effective grant of equal rights, would be admitted only grudgingly and incompletely, or only in theory but not in practice, and, if at all, hedged about with reservations and exceptions and continuing debate on its very advisability.

Further to the east and the south—which is to say, in the Russian and Ottoman Empires, in the independent states in the Balkans, and in those lands south of the Mediterranean that were still governed autonomously by indigenous rulers— the question of a grant of equality and full civil rights did not arise seriously at all. Not for the Jews—and not, of course, for anyone else. It was certainly not a question which the emperors, kings, sultans, beys, deys, and other potentates concerned, along with their ministers and advisers, thought they had cause seriously to consider. And, indeed, for a long while, their judgment was correct. Their own authority largely depended on the perpetuation—as opposed to a loosening and a liberalization—of the highly stratified, authoritarian society they controlled and were still able to manipulate with some success. A general grant of civil rights would have assuredly meant the death of their regimes, which is to say their own political death, and, conceivably, their own biological death as well. But there could certainly be no emancipation of the Jews without an emancipation of all or most of their other subjects. Accordingly, these were lands in which, for the time being, no emancipation of the Jews could be anticipated or projected at all.

Only a full century later, after the First World War, when in the subsequent general turmoil the old-style rulers along with their bureaucracies and satraps were indeed finally blown away, did Western-style (which is to say, French-style) emancipation become—or seem to become—a real possibility. Even then, the key word here is "possibility." While the ostensibly modern and forward-looking successors of the old rulers struck fresh political poses and their grounds for asserting their own authority and their methods of exercising it were generally new, by and large (with certain honorable exceptions) their regimes and policies turned out to be hardly less restrictive than those of their predecessors, so far as their Jewish subjects were concerned. In some cases these were more so. The period between the world wars was marked by the briefest of springs, followed by a long winter of deliberate efforts almost everywhere in Europe to cut down, even wholly abrogate, such civil rights as Jews had been granted either spontaneously by short-lived democratic governments or under heavy and exceedingly unwelcome pressure from abroad. All of which is abundantly illustrated by the rise of explicitly anti-Semitic regimes in newly independent Poland, in amputated Hungary, and in grossly enlarged Romania.

In any event, when, upon the outbreak of the Second World War, the Jews of Europe, from the Atlantic all the way to the western provinces of Russia, were herded back into the ghettos and very much worse, the process of emancipation may be said to have been totally reversed. It had been of exceedingly short duration. Its benefits were limited. Its legacy was ambiguous. What can be said of it with real confidence, however, is that it had done much to deprive the Jewish people of one of the foundations of its very long-standing, underlying stability and coherence by causing great numbers of its various components and divisions—its various communities—to differ ever more sharply one from the other according to the regime to which they were subject and the status accorded them. And from the resulting disparities two major, interlocking consequences for all Jewry *as a collectivity* resulted.

The first had to do with social and national attitudes. One might say, too: with attitudes to social and national issues. In the West, as doors opened, however slowly and grudgingly, it was clear that they were opening to *individuals*. It followed, for those who wished to take advantage of the opening and promote its extension, that an alternative to the ancient, explicitly *national* structure and conception of Jewry had to be devised. The prospect of continued isolation within the host society seemed not only ever less necessary, but ever less tolerable and ever less possible to sustain. And with what was rapidly becoming a great sea-change in the approach of Western Jews to their fundamental condition and to their relations with the surrounding peoples, they began to acquire the habit of examining themselves and their affairs very much less in traditional terms and by traditional criteria, very much more in the terms, and by the criteria, posed by others, and too with eyes which were becoming exceptionally—I would say, excessively—alert to the faults which *others* tended to ascribe to them. For an ever greater number of Jews, it became exceedingly important not simply to be left alone or be tolerated by their non-Jewish neighbors, but to be approved of by them; and the psychic consequences of this inversion were not infrequently disastrous, as much for individuals as for entire communities. "In the midst of German life is an alien and isolated race of men. Loud and self-conscious in their dress, hot-blooded and restless in their manner. An Asiatic horde on the sandy plains of Prussia."[8] Thus Walther Rathenau, the only German Jew to rise to a position of real power both in imperial and Weimar Germany, on the community into which he was born and from which he at no time sought seriously to escape.

In the East, no such open doors beckoned, or hardly any. Not only were the regimes harsher, but the general hostility was only very rarely diluted by some of that civility and restraint which, periods of crisis apart, tended to mitigate the social impact of anti-Jewish pressure in the west and (until the rise of the harsher forms of twentieth-century nationalism) greatly soften, if not virtually rule out, direct, physical harassment. And yet, in certain respects—until the organization by Germany of total catastrophe—Jewish society was stronger and substantially more stable than elsewhere. Language, social compactness, customs, political situation, patterns of economic life, culture, varieties of religious behavior, and indeed to a large degree social attitudes and tendencies and "mentality" in general—all these contributed to its internal strength and coherence.

While far from free in the full political sense—but on the contrary subject, notably in prerevolutionary Russia and later in the post-1918 successor states, to a multitude of restrictive laws, customs and social and economic barriers—the flip side of eastern European Jewry's defined and separate status was a measure of real internal autonomy. Accordingly, as they confronted large social questions, their cast of mind was not nearly so far removed from that of their ancestors as was that of their brethren in the West. They were largely untroubled by their social and political—let alone religious—isolation. They knew perfectly well that, when all was said and done, it had not been entirely forced on them. So far as most eastern European Jews were concerned, it was a fact of life, but by no

24

means an awkward or unwelcome one. In itself, it was not one
to be complained about or resisted as unnatural. It is thoroughly characteristic of Russo-Polish Jewry in this period that
as cracks appeared in the ancient walls of language, thought,
and culture that had done so much to render a national existence possible and coherent even in the most adverse of circumstances, so ever-increasing energy was mobilized in the
interests of their repair through a renewal and a reinvigoration
of national literature, art, and historiography. If there was any
kind of alternative on their horizon to what, by any standard,
was their coherent *national* existence, relatively few chose it and
fewer still looked to it really happily and with confidence. In
the main, the Jews of eastern Europe (and those of the Islamic
lands too) continued to examine their condition and their
surroundings from the inside looking out—which is not to
say that what they saw was in itself either encouraging or
satisfactory.

All in all, it is no kind of exaggeration to say that in all significant respects eastern European Jewry formed a *nation*—
one of the many, constituent nations of the region, one of the
class that were once termed "submerged" (meaning, essentially, nonsovereign, politically powerless) nations. True, it
was not the full Jewish nation. It was not congruent with the
entire, far-flung Jewish people. Yet it was far and away not
only the largest segment of it, but the one most given to seeing
itself and defining its interests and conducting its affairs in
national terms. If any sense can be made of the exceedingly
untidy structure of Jewry as it evolved and expanded right
through the nineteenth century and up until the outbreak of
the Second World War in the twentieth, and if anything like a
useful analytical order can be imposed upon it, then it is firmly

in its eastern European concentration that the essential body and center of gravity of the Jewish people—the torso, as opposed to the limbs, as it were—must be located. It is thus that these matters were most commonly understood at the time. It is thus that they can best be seen and rendered intelligible in retrospect. By the same token it was on the fate of eastern European Jewry, more than on any other single factor or fraction of Jewry, that the destinies of modern Jewry as a whole have hinged. So long as it held together, the rest of Jewry, no matter how secure, prosperous, and socially energetic particular communities turned out to be, no matter how worthy and celebrated leading individual members of other communities may have been, no matter how great the influence they brought to bear and the contribution they made to the management of supracommunal affairs—all this, all the rest, constituted periphery. Compared with the great mass of Russo-Polish Jewry, along with its outlying branches in Romania and Hungary, the rest of the Jewish world was an untidy, ill-connected congeries of communities, some fully coherent and tightly run, others so loose and ill-defined and ragged at the edges as to raise the question whether they were part of a Jewish world, however that might be defined and however that might be conceived. It is of course perfectly true that the Jews of eastern Europe came increasingly to depend on their remote brethren for material help and even to rely somewhat on the instruments and institutions of political action which could function in relative freedom in the West, but which they themselves were incapable of establishing and operating. In this respect, as in some others, the relationship between periphery and center came to be somewhat analogous to one which other nations developed between their emigrant and exilic communities on the one hand and their root population in the country of origin on the other. Naturally enough, so long as the center more or less held together, such leadership as the periphery offered proved to be only partly acceptable, if at all. As the center collapsed, such material and political assistance as was on offer from the periphery proved hopelessly, pitifully, bitterly inadequate, making the underlying structure fully manifest.

In our own times, the apparent, yet in many ways paradoxical, successor to the great eastern European concentration is Israel: the Jewish community in Israel, one might say. It is paradoxical because, while the Zionists as the national movement *par excellence* were flesh of their flesh and the sources and *raison d'être* of Zionism both as a creed and as a program were firmly rooted in eastern Europe, Zionism itself could never claim more than a large minority of its people as true supporters—a larger minority than in other parts of the Jewish world, but a minority nonetheless. The traditionalists of religious orthodoxy, the socialists (notably the Bundists), the autonomists, and, of course, the assimilationists in their virtually infinite variety of degrees of acculturation and identification—all these together substantially outnumbered them. Yet Israel, whatever it may have now become, is very much the creation—the daughter, the colony, so to speak—of eastern European, notably Russo-Polish Jews and cannot be understood historically, or interpreted politically and ideologically, without close attention being paid to its origins in Odessa, Warsaw, Vilna, Minsk, Berdichev, and the many other centers of Jewish life in the age before and between the world wars. Of course, to say this is no more than to underline the immense disparity in ethos, structure, and culture between Israel as one

of the great branches of contemporary Jewry and all others—
so great a disparity and so central a constituent element of the
contemporary crisis in Jewry as to require separate treatment,
such as will follow.

For the second broad consequence of the growing disparity
between the post-1789 fates of Western as opposed to all
other Jewries ran more deeply still and may, perhaps, prove to
be more lasting. It has less to do with circumstances directly,
however, than with what people have learned from their immediate circumstances and made of them—and not merely in
an observational way, but rather in a more fundamental and
philosophical sense. It has to do with general outlook on life,
on mankind, on society, and on Providence—in a word, with
Weltanschauung.

TWO

The Transformation of Jewry and the Confusion of the National Interest

Even the most cursory review of the recent history of the Jewish people reveals both extraordinary intensity of change and an accelerated rate of change. In the course of less than a century the Jewish people has been transformed demographically, socially, culturally, and—perhaps most profoundly of all—politically. There has been the great migration from east to west and the consolidation of the American Jewish community, which, despite its relative lack of unity, coherence, and effective leadership (let alone direction), remains not only the most numerous, but the most vigorous, the freest, and easily the most powerful segment of the contemporary Jewish Diaspora. There has been the destruction of eastern and central European Jewry at the hands of Germany, in the shadow of which catastrophe it seems we still live—without being fully capable as yet of taking its true measure and drawing useful operative conclusions. There has been throughout this period an exceedingly powerful, some might think overwhelming, wave of secularization and assimilation to other cultures, societies, and nations such that no artificial heightening of "Jewish consciousness," no effort to serve up the grinding misery of the Russo-Polish *shtetl* (hamlet) in jolly musical-comedy terms, and no campaign to render the modern, secular, urban, Euro-American Jew *pious* after the manner of his great-great-grand-father will ever reverse. And there has been the achievement of political independence and sovereignty by what can be usefully thought of, for present purposes, as the modern Jewish community of, first Palestine, now Israel. The ways in which these great social and political developments were related to each other and have at various times and in various ways either enhanced or diminished each other's impact form the chief matter of modern Jewish history. In our times, at all events, towards the end of the terrible twentieth century, it is surely the last, the successful establishment of a sovereign Israel, which has come to color, if not to overshadow, all else. It is the source of greatest expectations and deepest concern—not least because it was an event the full and long-term significance of which none, either in Israel or elsewhere, either in the Jewish world or outside it, can yet grasp. As with the Holocaust, nei-ther Jews or non-Jews (apart perhaps, and for obvious reasons, from members of the Muslim world) know quite what to make of it and how to live with it, if at all.

But before coming directly to this, the central theme of the present essay, it is worth noting that in step with all these other developments, and partly as their consequence, the situation and status of the Jews relative to those of other peoples have changed in very important respects. It may be said of the Jews today that they have moved much closer to center stage in international politics. They no longer merely constitute a "problem" or "question" in the old sense, a topic to be consid-ered only when absolutely necessary or as a sop to petitioners, and then only as a dossier to be taken out, flipped through, and returned to the archives as soon as possible and with relief, before passing on to other matters.

In the contemporary light of day the Jews have been revealed as no more, but no less, than a moderately important, active, independent, if still unusual factor in their own right whose main trump card is the one which in the past they were least suspected of possessing, let alone knowing how to exploit: the military. Strictly speaking, the use of the military card, along with other instruments of (sovereign) policy, is, of course, the prerogative of the Israeli branch of Jewry. But it is precisely on that use—actual, but equally potential—and on the unfamiliar phenomenon of national sovereignty itself that the central dilemmas of Jewry as a whole, within Israel but also outside it, largely turn.

The profundity of the sea-change that has come over both the Jews themselves and the manner in which they are perceived by others is best brought out by a glance back at the former state of affairs. It may be illustrated by the considered judgment of one Jean Gout, a well-informed, thoroughly competent, senior official at the Quai d'Orsay who had occasion to comment (for the benefit of his superiors) on the Jewish national-political tendency, and on Zionism in particular, just as it was finally emerging into the full political light of day. The time was May 1917. The Great War was at its frightful, murderous peak; but moved by the (February) revolution in Russia and the advance of Allenby's forces in the Levant, the thoughts of the professionals of diplomacy were as much on the future as on the present.

The millenary aspirations of the Jews, especially of the proletarians of Poland and Russia, are neither socialist, as their social

31

situation would lead to believe, nor nationalist, as the declarations of their intellectuals claim. Essentially they are Talmudic, which is to say religious. The legends which have served to soothe the misery of these poor devils have made them see a restored Jerusalem as the end of all their ills, Paradise on earth where the God of Israel would reign in triumph . . .

One should not exaggerate the import of these dreams, but neither should they be thoughtlessly disparaged. Even after attaining positions of distinction in countries of civil equality, intelligent and educated Jews retain the dream of the ancient ghettos in a corner of their hearts for several generations. Thanks to their wealth, the ties they maintain among themselves, and the influence they bring to bear on ignorant governments, they do carry a certain international weight. But they are not and cannot be a *factor*. A wise policy would [therefore] allow the Jews to envisage the possibility of [Jewish] association in Palestine, but within the limits of existing nationalities, and not as an independent one.[1]

The old myth of international Jewish power has long since died (except perhaps in some corners of the Arab world and, it seems, in certain important segments of black society in the United States). It was killed, one supposes, by the Germans who did so much to exploit it. Even the Russians, for all their efforts in our own times, have failed to revive it, at all events effectively and for anyone who gives serious thought to such matters. Equally, the Jews have ceased to be—notably for those who, with no regard for the implicit contradiction, perversely thought of them as all-powerful—that mysterious, immensely capable, but secretive people, equipped with powers of manipulation in all the major departments of human affairs. What has replaced the old myth is a contemporary truth of substantially more modest, but also more real power. Today the Jews are a *facteur,* as the French diplomat quoted rightly perceived they were not in 1917. There is now better knowledge of the Jews all round—of their strengths, their weaknesses, their qualities, their faults—knowledge of the Jews, warts and all, knowledge of the Jews as real people or virtually so. Better knowledge of them than in earlier times and, in some quarters, a measure of sympathy and understanding, along with, in other quarters, or even the same quarters, much irritation and impatience of a wholly new kind; and some fear too that, in ways still undefined, these peculiar people will end by upsetting the international applecart and serve, as the trite phrase goes, as a catalyst, perhaps *the* catalyst, of the great world conflagration all thinking people dread. In a word, the Jews are now mostly seen correctly, as they were once seen incorrectly, as being part of the real world of power and politics, their power-political role having been confirmed and made inescapable by the prolonged, declared, and active hostility of the Soviet Union, of most of the Muslim world, and of important members of the rest of the Third World, but also, in the final analysis, by the brute fact of Israel's existence. The result has been to involve the Jews in international politics willy-nilly, and precisely where the fight is thickest.

But it is to the internal aspects of the change, rather than the familiar external and international aspects of the reentry of the Jews into the political arena—into "history" one is tempted to say—that this essay is addressed. "Internal"? The term itself raises questions. Is modern Jewry in fact a coherent society, let alone a nation, of which it is proper to speak in all-embracing language, with an "inside" and an "outside," with *boundaries?* I shall come back to this, for the matter of the terms in which it

33

is proper and reasonable to speak of "Jewry" (itself an extremely loose and, for that very reason, a particularly convenient concept) is a crucial part of the current predicament. But first, why should it be posited that there is a predicament at all?

As a general rule, few men of good will would deny the contention that among the greatest of social questions in—and for—all societies is the question whether the dictates of morality upon us are compatible—or can be rendered compatible—with our political and material interests as best we understand them. Pragmatists and out-and-out moralists would say that this, at the very minimum, is the question whether what is imperative on the plane of morality is practicable on the plane of interest—but different schools would, of course, weight the scales differently. Still, most of us, in practice and whatever our views on specific issues might be, would surely prefer to be shown that the ancient and familiar dilemmas of *raison d'état* and the related, equally ancient and familiar political dichotomies of right and force and of ends and means can be largely, even if not entirely, resolved. Accordingly, even among skeptics, there is some natural sympathy for one well-established method of setting out to show how the difficult trick of reconciling the two may be performed. And there would be much more sympathy for it were its popularity not so great among precisely those people who might be expected to see its weaknesses most clearly.

The method in question may be summed up as the resolution of these, the greatest and most fundamental of political dilemmas, by showing that it is in the *interest* of those concerned to pursue a moral course—because, for example, the political climate in which contemporary statesmen operate in particular international conflicts is in any event such as to ease the situation of the moral party and incommode the immoral one. To pragmatists who remind the moralists of the fate which actually attended the most famous of modern attempts to reduce political interest to moral principle, the response can and will be made that from his day to our own, Woodrow Wilson's purposes have never been pursued with anything but faintheartedness and that they have still to be properly tested. Besides, it will be said, Wilson the man was his own worst enemy.

> He was not only insensitive to his surroundings in the external sense [wrote Lord Keynes], he was not sensitive to his environment at all. What chance could such a man have against Mr. Lloyd George's unerring, almost medium-like, sensibility to everyone immediately around him? . . . Never could a man have stepped into the parlour a more perfect and predestined victim of the finished accomplishments of the Prime Minister. The Old World was tough in wickedness anyhow; the Old World's heart of stone might blunt the sharpest blade of the bravest knight errant. This blind and deaf Don Quixote was entering a cavern where the swift and glittering blade was in the hands of the adversary.[2]

But in any case, the argument continues, the ways of today's political world are not the ways of the world of 1917–1919: just as it was among Wilson's errors to be ahead of his time, so it would be our error to be behind the times seven decades later.

These terrible moral and intellectual dilemmas—and political dilemmas too, of course—spring first and foremost from the sheer *ability* to act politically and employ force in your own interest when you possess it. These being dilemmas that the Jewish people had not been accustomed to confront, it is not

35

surprising that until quite recent times most Jews (in common, be it said, with many other men of good will) wanted to believe that the well-known dilemmas of *raison d'état* and ends and means were largely, if not entirely, capable of resolution. In international politics, at any rate, most Jews tended to be distant if unconscious followers of Woodrow Wilson. They believed, that is to say, that the trick could be done and the dilemmas resolved by learning to see (and showing others) that it was generally in one's *interest* to follow a moral course—morality being conceived in traditional private terms. They believed, too, that in any particular conflict the interests of the various competing groups could always, ultimately, be rendered compatible one with the other. They believed, finally, that the moral course of action—dissolved by the righteous into the expedient one—could almost always be identified. Certainly this, or something along these lines, was what intelligent, informed, well-meaning members of the various Jewish communities—in Palestine/Israel, no less than anywhere else—tended to think and tended not to question. It is still what very many passionately wish to believe, as we shall see. And if today (to put the point very cautiously) the evidence is that some in Jewry are a little wiser, it is a piece of wisdom that many more find exceedingly distasteful. Or to put the matter somewhat differently again, there are those who do not wish under any circumstances to accept the sour fruit of recent experience as having operative significance for themselves—for themselves as Jews, at any rate. Or to put it in yet another but rougher form, if worldly wisdom is what must now inform the Jewish world, now that the Jews too are equipped with a state machine, with fully declared enemies, and, worst of all, are to be found in a position of local political and military dominance over others, then many will (and indeed do) say: So much the worse for worldly wisdom and so much the worse for the State and its problems. We would rather do without them; we would rather have back our former innocence and impregnable moral position. Weakness and vulnerability, many will say, have their virtues; and for that reason, if for no other, their attractions.

This "neo-Wilsonian" view of the matter corresponds roughly, but significantly enough, to what a noted psychologist, following William James, has categorized as the "tender-minded" (as opposed to the "tough-minded")[3] approach to politics. This is not to say that it does not deserve some sympathy. Who would want to quarrel with those who, as they survey the world, note unhappily the endless proliferation of social and political causes whose inner truth and vitality are measured in the minds of their respective adherents by nothing more than that which the late Ya'akov Talmon, a most perceptive historian of the modern era, once termed "audacity and ruthlessness in the use of violence and cruelty"?[4] But the causes of the steadily widening gulf between the tender- and the tough-minded in contemporary Jewry run much more deeply than their respective responses to what they read in their morning newspapers.

In the contemporary West, generally speaking, respect for the rights of man and the citizen, the rule of law, certain well-tried methods of patient, peaceful resolution of conflict by negotiation—all these and more have come to be seen not only as immensely desirable in themselves and infinitely preferable to other, darker principles, techniques, and instruments

37

of social and political action, but as actually in evidence, and if not all the time, then much of the time. They operate, they are available, and, all things considered, are maintained in fairly good repair. And of the application of these principles and the workings of the accompanying institutions in practice, the Jews of western Europe, and now of North America too, have been among the notable beneficiaries. What could be more natural, then, than their evident attachment to a view of society and its troubles, and of likely solutions to those troubles, which is intrinsically optimistic, altruistic, moralistic, and so, by extension, legalistic too, but above all principled? How, at a deeper level, could such a view, if it is to be sustained, fail to be profoundly dismissive of the opposing outlook: that which holds that, in important ways, men (and women) are often irretrievably at cross-purposes with each other and that, in this vale of tears, evil is endemic and ineradicable?

For there *is* another outlook. To the east and to the south of the fortunate lands of northwest Europe and North America, things were, and have long remained, otherwise—and not for the Jews alone, but for all. And there is no need to recite even a reduced catalogue of the afflictions which have overcome virtually all the peoples of central and eastern Europe, of the Middle East and Central Asia, of both northern and sub-Saharan Africa, and of southern Asia and the Far East in our own times and before our eyes.

The world outside the West is a hard world. The lessons it offers are hard, too. In the lands in which violence, cruelty, tyranny, and hatred are endemic, there is good reason to conclude that safety is unlikely to lie in reliance on the rules of law and common morality, let alone the native decency and good will of individual men and women. One tends easily and naturally to skepticism, to distrust, and therefore, so far as possible, to self-reliance. In a hard world, it is prudent to learn (and follow) hard lessons.

The result has been that, in the course of time, different communities of Jews can be seen ever more clearly not only to have become very differently placed, but to have tended increasingly to inhabit different mental and philosophical worlds. And it is not only the profundity of some of the differences, but their actual quality that creates barriers to understanding and cooperation. For the issues over which the division is now greatest have to do not so much, as in the past, with traditional law, or ritual (over which there are divisions too, but of a lesser order), but with the aims, methods, and even the propriety of collective action by Jews—above all, if by no means exclusively, when collective action relies on the autonomous, political employment of instruments of influence and power.

Seen in the perspective offered by the full sweep of Jewish history, this is an ominous development. Nothing is so divisive as an idea that pertains at one and the same time both to interest and to propriety: to what is desirable *and* to what is right. In the final analysis, the real profundity of the revolution the Emancipation helped to precipitate in Jewish life is revealed less in the differences between the material and formal-legal circumstances of the various sectors of the Jewish people than in the philosophical, ideological, and psychic qualities that tend now to divide them. The heat of contemporary arguments about both interest and propriety—in effect, the central internal debate in contemporary Jewry—is so great, the tone so bitter, and the prospect of a meeting of minds so remote,

39

that the notion that the long era of Jewish unity across many frontiers, always somewhat tenuous, but always real, is finally about to end seems subject to continual reinforcement.

The division between the schools is by no means congruent—certainly not precisely congruent—with the division of Jewry into Israelis and non-Israelis. Tender-minded neo-Wilsonians are not in the least rare in Israel. They can be found and seen and heard daily and in substantial numbers there, the more so as, by and large, it is they who have the advantage of the better press both at home and abroad. This, in turn, has had much to do with their having proved exceedingly articulate—far more so than any of their rivals. But it has had no less to do with the fact that, by and large, what they have actually had to say is what most Jews outside Israel (and of course many, many others outside Jewry) would like to hear: that the Arab-Israeli conflict could and would be wound down if only there were a sufficiency of good will; that there *is* good reason to negotiate with the Arabs, notably with the leaders of the PLO; that there *are* Arabs (in the PLO itself, no less than elsewhere) with whom one can effectively and not too dangerously negotiate; and, finally, that for all these reasons it is plainly as much the fault of *Israel* (at any rate of its government and *classe politique*) no less than, if latterly not more than, the fault of the Arabs that no end to the conflict is yet in sight, that there seems to be no light at all at the end of the dark and depressing tunnels through which the people of Israel and their immediate neighbors have been moving virtually throughout the twentieth century.

But the internal debate within Israel is just that: an internal debate. However fierce and bitter, it is a debate of a kind for which the history of modern sovereign states offers innumerable precedents and which is bound, like all others, to be settled sooner or later, one way or another, either by a process of internal political decision or by the full impact of events over which the state has no control, or, most likely of all, by a combination of both. In contrast, the parallel debate between the schools of tough- and tender-minded, of pragmatists and moralists, as it is pursued across *all* of Jewry, while it turns, nominally, on much the same issues, is fundamentally of a very different order. In some ways it is less open and frank. In other but related ways it is fueled by even greater bitterness. What is most important is that it is the source of what must now be the most acute of the many tensions which have been building up within Jewry in recent years. It demonstrates—not least by the fact that in the *world* Jewish context it is an issue that cannot be decided one way or the other—that in regard to the Jewish people's capacity for dealing effectively with the great political purposes, questions, and interests that concern it, the nature and structure of contemporary Jewry is profoundly fractured and dysfunctional. Issues which touch upon political relations between Jewry and other peoples are a particular case in point.

A Jewish diplomat—if one has in mind a person or functionary analogous to an English diplomat, a French, or American, or Russian, or Japanese diplomat—implies a Jewish diplomacy. That in turn, if one excludes mere intercession by one well-placed element or member of Jewry on behalf of another, less well-placed, implies a Jewish interest: a Jewish *collective* interest; some would say, a Jewish national interest. But combine the terms and speak of a Jewish national diplomacy, or diplomacy in the Jewish interest, and two things are immediately clear: that there has been nothing remotely like it since the onset of the Exile until very recent times; and that even

41

today it is by no means clear what it could or should signify, or even whether, in a strict sense, there can be such a function at all. Even in our own times, let alone fifty or a hundred years ago, it is an open question whether there is in any material (which is to say social, economic, and political-organizational) sense a Jewish collectivity. There may be strong views on the subject. There may be myths. There may be intentions. There may even be dreams. But the reality of Jewish life remains complex and protean. Jewry has no formal boundaries; its informal boundaries are subject to constant movement, change, and debate. There is no person, group, or institution competent to represent it in its entirety, let alone capable of doing so in practice, because, of course, there is no central authority governing it. But more: there is no agreement about what constitutes the Jewish national interest, or what could constitute it, or how it might be determined, or even what might serve as the major elements and points of reference upon which such a determination would be based. Nor indeed could this exercise be satisfactorily performed and agreement achieved (for who would constitute the forum which would pronounce upon it?) without doing violence to the central facts of Jewish life. And these, today, having regard to the present context, are four in number.

Firstly, Jews, however we may wish to define them, live under two sharply divided and distinct regimes: some live under a Jewish government which purports (by no means improperly, it should be said) to be pursuing Jewish national purposes; others live under governments which may or may not include individual Jews in their higher reaches, but certainly do not, indeed may not, pursue any but the purposes of the nations they rule and claim to represent. Governments, the

Jewish government among them, have powers of compulsion.
The great majority of Jews in Israel bear loyalty to their government. The great majority of Jews elsewhere bear loyalty to
other governments.

Secondly, Jews in all parts are profoundly divided among
themselves on the matter of Judaism itself—its content, its
validity, its interpretation, and its contemporary relevance and
value. The fundamental division is, of course, between believers
and freethinkers. The subsidiary but hardly less important division is between, on the one hand, those for whom the Jewish
past is cardinal both for its intrinsic value and as a guide for the
contemporary perplexed and, on the other hand, those for
whom there is much in the past that deserves to be rejected in
principle and, so far as it survives in our own times, to be
shaken off in practice.

Thirdly, the Jews are subject to cultural differences and divisions which go beyond (but may to some extent explain) the
different regimes to which they are subject and their differences on the matter of Judaism itself. If one takes the term
"culture" in a very loose, but, I think, useful sense, Jewry is
partly European, at least at one or two removes, and partly
non-European. "Europe," for present purposes, may be said
to include North America and the Antipodes. Whether it
includes America south of the Rio Grande I am not competent
to say; but it does not, except to a limited and diminishing
degree, include Israel.

Fourthly, the Jews are divided ideologically on the great and
immensely difficult issue which plainly underlies the subject
of this essay. I have in mind the conversion of the Jews—the
reconversion, one might say with equal justice—into a political
people. The chief engine of this process of reconversion has

43

been the Zionist movement; and the process itself has been intensified and accelerated by that still more powerful force, sovereign Israel. It is more powerful because the circumstances of Israel, its conflict with the Arab states, its further involvement in the East-West conflict, its striking series of military victories and political defeats, its decades-long location at the center of one of the great international whirlpools of our times (into which Jews everywhere have been sucked to some extent), and the fear, the love, the hatred, the admiration, and the dislike it evokes variously and sometimes simultaneously—all these have tended to involve the Jews outside Israel, and beyond its formal jurisdiction, in its affairs; in spirit and in fact, for good and for ill. The government of Israel therefore sustains a relationship with world Jewry to which none of the accepted and conventional political categories are applicable, for which there are no true precedents, and which evokes joy, dismay, comfort, and dread—again, variously and sometimes simultaneously—as the case may be: too weak and indeterminate a relationship for some, too strong and binding a relationship for others.

So it appears. Is it so in fact? Is the "centrality" of Israel a true fact of Jewish life, as opposed to being a principle which some hold, while others (with, if anything, greater vehemence) deny? On the face of it, the evidence is abundant. Academic investigators speak of a "Jewish civil religion," at the very foundation of which lies regard (to use no stronger term) for Israel. Successive crises in the Middle East have irritated and frightened non-Israelis as often as they have heartened them. Still, the passion of the response in either case may be taken as the measure of the degree to which the eyes of world Jewry are now consistently upon Israel, a Mecca to which most Jews, if they do not all make pilgrimage, do tend to make a form—admittedly an exceedingly mild form—of obeisance. Reform Judaism, once strident in its objection to Zionism and to the notion of Jewish political autonomy, is now, by and large, sympathetic. A "task force" organized some years ago by that supremely cautious and respectable institution, the American Jewish Committee, to consider the "interaction" between Israel and the American Jewish community, even went so far as to resolve *inter alia* that "the State of Israel has a crucial role in the future of the Jewish people" and that "the Israeli and American Jewish communities share an agenda of common concern that requires reciprocal and mutual determination."[5] It could hardly have gone further without undermining its own moral position and social authority in the United States—not, at all events, without a change of heart so radical as to entail a complete reversal of position and a discrediting of all it had traditionally stood for. Jews who dislike most or all of what recent, preponderantly "right-wing"—in fact, populist-provincial—governments of Israel have stood for, Jews who were never happy about the establishment of an independent state in the first place, and even Jews who, to this day, are firm in their public protestation of exclusive loyalty to the country of their domicile—all these and other categories and classes in that amorphous social entity we term world Jewry, with only marginal exceptions, feel bound to declare an attachment of some kind to the land and the people and even to the State of Israel, at least in principle. Others, of course, reject Israel and all its works (and most of its people) out of hand. But if, qualitatively, the exceptions (chiefly in the ultra-orthodox and the ultra-left and universalist wings of Jewry) are of interest and importance, statistically they verge on the peripheral. So far as the majority are concerned, the louder and more public the criticism of the government and society of Israel, the warmer, generally speaking, are the terms in which the bond with the people of Israel and the (new-found) loyalty to the ideas, true or imagined, on which it was *originally* founded are evoked.

Why this should be so is an important and interesting question; but it is not one to which I propose to address myself in this essay. This is partly because of its complexity, because, plainly, there is no single or simple answer to it, which is to say no answer that can be usefully discussed in such limited compass as the present one. And partly, it is because I believe it is too early in time, too soon historically, to arrive at a clear view of the matter. Too much is still in flux. But chiefly it is because what should, to my mind, be of immediate and urgent concern is the issue which arises as a *practical* consequence of the new post-1948 circumstances. And these circumstances are that, on the one hand, Jewry is subject to unprecedented divisions of the kind to which I have already alluded; and, on the other hand, it now has within it, as one of its principal components, a political force and authority which has assumed (or should one say, presumes to) something approaching overall leadership, a leadership to which no other force or body can conceivably—or does in fact—lay claim.

The fundamental issue that arises has two parts or two faces which may, I believe, be defined thus. There is, in the first place, the question to what extent, and in what sense, policy made by the government of Israel is in fact and in principle policy for Jewry as a whole. In the second place, it is what the further consequences of this new state of affairs might be for the various classes and communities of Jews in Israel itself and outside it, but chiefly in Israel. I add the caveat "chiefly in

Israel" because the concerns and outlook of the Jews of the Diaspora cannot be those of the Jews in Israel, except indirectly and somewhat unnaturally and by a special effort of empathy. It is with their own society and polity that the Jews of Israel are directly (and properly) concerned; and there is no doubt that it is their own very particular circumstances that largely shape their outlook on this as on other matters. Therein lies the problem.

The central fact of Jewish public life today, some forty years after 1948, is that what is done, what is intended, and equally what is said by the relevant authorities in Israel all impinge not only upon the lives and fortunes of its citizens, but directly and indirectly, in one degree or another, on the lives and fortunes and expectations of the members of other Jewish communities. Such is the case, by and large, no matter how remote they may be from us (in Israel) in space, in culture, in material circumstances, in concerns, and, indeed, in terms of their own specific interests as they themselves understand them.

It follows that the policies—I have external and defense policies in mind in the first place, but also public policy in the sphere of personal status, the regulation of marriage and divorce and the like—pursued by a government of Israel, whatever its complexion, tend strongly to be regarded as policies of, at all events for, the Jewish people as a whole; and that there are not wholly unreasonable grounds for so regarding them. It is certainly the case that many in Israel and outside it, Jews and non-Jews, friends and enemies, would so argue. The policies of Israel may be policies for all Jewry only very imperfectly—as would accord with the imperfect, ill-defined, and uncertain nature of the ties and mutual obligations that obtain between Israel and the Jewish Diaspora. There may be a thou-

47

sand exceptions to what is, anyway, less a rule than a blanket characterization. But the entanglement of Jewry in all its variety of condition, belief, and desire in the affairs of Israel—which is to say, in the Zionist enterprise in its contemporary stage— is now beyond dispute and, most probably, beyond unscrambling. And the upshot has been that Jewry has taken on an increasingly national aspect: "national" in a sense that ostensibly accords with what is commonly accepted and expected of nations, which is to say, a political sense. The causes are complex. In part, they derive from the enormous injuries to body and spirit suffered by the Jews in this century. In part, the phenomenon represents the triumph of Zionism. It was precisely this possibility that the most determined critics of Zionism had always objected to and had always feared. When, in October 1917, the president of the Anglo-Jewish Association, C. G. Montefiore, was asked by the British government for his views on the draft of what later became the Balfour Declaration, he replied:

> I deprecate the expression "a national home." For it assumes that the Jewish race constitutes a "nation," or might profitably become a nation, both of which propositions I deny. The phrase "a national home for the Jewish race" appears to assume and imply that the Jews generally constitute a nationality. Such an implication is extremely prejudicial to Jewish interests, as it is intensely obnoxious to an enormous number of Jews. There can be no objection to Jews who *want* to form themselves into a nationality going to Palestine and forming themselves into a nationality in that country, but it must be effected without any prejudice to the character and position of the Jews as nationals of other countries.[6]

48

But how does Israel, as a sovereign state among other sovereign states, affect the lives and fortunes of non-Israeli Jews in actual practice? Broadly, there are three ways in which Israeli diplomacy—using the term "diplomacy" in its looser sense, namely the management of the country's foreign relations—impinges on the Jewish Dispersion. The first, most obviously and directly, is as a function of the ever wider sweep of the Arab-Israeli conflict: international terrorism and counterterror, economic sanctions and pressure, and, in a general way, the ever-greater felt need of all those who are nominally on the sidelines to take a public position on the issue. These include Jews, Christians, Muslims, the political left, the political right, anti-Semites, philo-Semites, intellectuals, men- and women-in-the-street, political leaders of nations which are geographically and psychologically remote from the eastern Mediterranean, hardly less than of those with a real stake in the outcome, and of course the men and women of the mass media. Who, today, stands aside? Who remains silent when he (or she) can plunge into the fray at little or no cost to himself, and often to his advantage? Who, preferring to be silent, does not in some measure regret it? The precise degree to which the deeds of Israel, and of those who act in its name, have served to create this atmosphere and continue to affect it is open to question. What cannot be denied is that the floodlights of world opinion are fully upon Israel and that whatever its government and/or its people do (as opposed, perhaps, to whatever is done to them) is liable to instant broadcast and magnification; and that the effect on Jews outside Israel has been severe. It may be that the process by which all Jewry is in one way or another entangled in the affairs of Israel and the Israelis is not yet at its

49

height; but it is clearly underway and has been gathering force for some years. Of all this the events of the latter half of 1982 consequent upon the war in Lebanon provided one great demonstration. The unexpectedly prolonged and violent rising of young Arabs in the occupied territories towards the end of 1987 (still in progress in 1990) has provided another.

The second way in which the diplomacy of Israel impinges heavily on the Jewish world as a whole pertains to the realm of belief, principle, and view of self. This is the realm of the intangible, the realm of dignity and, if one may use a term which some may think so old-fashioned as to be ridiculous, honor. By the same token, it is the realm of obligation. There is therefore much to be said about it, far too much for more than a hint of the immensity of the problem to be touched upon here and now. But it may not be neglected or merely referred to in passing, the more so as there has been one great issue which it is entirely appropriate to mention in the present context because it almost perfectly encapsulates both the specific question of national dignity and posture *and* the general topic of national diplomacy. I have in mind the demand for, and the acceptance of, reparations from Germany in the immediate aftermath of the destruction by Germany of European Jewry—the major part of the Jewish Diaspora as it was then constituted.

I do not propose to address myself directly to the question whether it was legitimate to make that demand, still less why those concerned at the time, namely the government of Israel and a group of Jewish notables representing the principal non-Israeli Jewish institutions, resolved to make it. That is a chapter in the history of the Jews that remains to be properly written, part of the larger, vastly more complex, vastly more painful

50

history of the Jewish people during the Second World War and in its immediate aftermath. When that is done it may finally be explained to us how it came about that the leaders and institutions concerned to press and negotiate the matter of the reparations were, for all intents and purposes, identical with those functioning *before* the war; how it was, in other words, after all that had happened to the Jews, that there was in Jewry no subsequent change of a *political* order, no great sweeping away of the old guard, no radical rethinking of the basis of Jewish life in the Diaspora, and that, with one salient exception, it was *continuity* that marked the Jews once more in all their public and collective affairs. Even that one great exception, the establishment of Israel, owed far more to the internal dynamic of the triangular Anglo-Arab-Jewish conflict in Palestine than to any other set of factors, not excluding the events of 1939–1945 in Europe. But one way or the other, it is instructive and, perhaps, characteristic that the first approach to the Allied Powers in the matter of German reparations (in 1945) was made by the Jewish Agency; and that it was followed up, as if in the normal course of events, by the new State of Israel five and a half years later.

The precise wording of Chaim Weizmann's formal Note of 1945 to the four Allied Powers is of great interest. For one of the questions that evidently arose in the minds of those who drafted it was that of their own *locus standi* in the matter. It was a major question in its own right; it was the first question they could expect to have put to them by those to whom they were applying. Who were these claimants? Whom did they represent? What grounds were there, what grounds could there be, for treating with them in a context which by all accepted criteria pertained exclusively to the familiar *personae* and protagonists

51

of international law, international relations, and diplomacy—namely recognized, sovereign states?

The answer given by Weizmann and his colleagues to the anticipated question was clear-cut. On "the problems of requiring Germany and her satellites in the measure of the practicable, to make good the losses they have inflicted," they stated, "the Jewish Agency for Palestine, as the representative of the Jewish people, desires to draw attention to that aspect of the problem which affects the Jewish people and in particular to their relation to Palestine."[7] Thus, explicitly: "the Jewish Agency, as the representative of the Jewish people." No formulation could be clearer. And therefore, perhaps, it was doomed from the first to be ignored by the Powers and to be dropped before long by the Agency itself, as well as by its successor, the government of Israel. Neither the Jewish Agency, nor the State of Israel, nor any one of the twenty institutions that constituted the Claims Conference, ranging from Agudat Israel to the World Jewish Congress and from the American Jewish Committee to the Alliance Israélite Universelle, was ever formally referred to again—or ever referred to itself again—as a representative of "the Jewish people." Israel's *locus standi* was said to rest on the part it played in the absorption and rehabilitation of the survivors of Germany's war against the Jews;[8] and it was for that very specific reason that Israel was entitled to economic support. The formal resolutions adopted by the Conference on Jewish Material Claims against Germany are notable for beginning with the qualifying statement that "this Conference was called together for the *sole* purpose of considering Jewish material claims against Germany."[9]

The final agreements signed at Luxembourg were drafted in the same spirit and say no more. This issue of representation was left open, unsettled and unstated. And yet: who would deny that in some sense, over and above the "material claims" presented and the material reparations agreed upon, a form of peace was concluded at Luxembourg between Jews and Germans? To be sure, it was no ordinary peace. It had been no ordinary conflict. The protagonists were not symmetrical, either in their conflict or in its resolution. On the German side, there was a conventionally and democratically constituted governmental body. On the Jewish side, the people on whose behalf and in whose name this peace was concluded had not been consulted and could not be consulted; and those who spoke for them were possessed of very unusual, not to say imperfect, credentials. It may be argued that there was here an arrogation of authority, the more extraordinary for no such authority being entirely plausible or possible even in theory. Yet the moral consequences for all of Jewry at the time, as well as for later generations, have been, and will remain, profound.

Could things have been otherwise? Surely all action on behalf of Jewry as a whole entails some such arrogation of authority? Are we to deny Weizmann, David Ben Gurion, Moshe Sharett, and Nahum Goldmann what we have retroactively condoned in Theodor Herzl? Or would Herzl and his contemporaries have acted differently in this particular case? Clear answers to such questions as these have never been forthcoming. It is not too much to say that they have never been properly and publicly debated.

The third way in which the management of the foreign relations of Israel impinges on the lives and fortunes of Jews who are neither residents nor citizens of the country is *political* in every sense of the term. It has a great deal to do with Israel's slender resources, political and other, and the effort which successive governments of that country have pursued to enlarge and enhance them. At its mildest, it is the welcome extended to pro-Israel circles in other countries which offer spontaneous help and encouragement. At its strongest, and at its most controversial, it is the deliberate, if necessarily cautious, recruitment and encouragement of such circles and the attempt to guide them into politically effective and profitable channels. Such circles, leaders of opinion, churches, societies, and so forth need not be Jewish, and often are not. Insofar as they are not, they differ in no way from such friends and resources as any one nation may seek legitimately to have within the body politic of another. But where they are Jewish, in whole or in part, matters are otherwise; so too when the grounds for support by non-Jews are, at least ostensibly, reducible to (and contingent upon) likely Jewish sympathy or pressure and a desire to accommodate it. The power and influence of such pro-Israel lobbies vary from place to place and from time to time. The demonic, power-hungry qualities ascribed to them by Arab politicians openly, and by a surprisingly large number of Western diplomats and journalists more or less privately, have no basis in fact. But it would be absurd to say that they are devoid of power and influence altogether, and entirely ridiculous to suggest that they have made no attempt to garner influence and, in the event, apply it. What does seem clear is that such influence as they can bring to bear has tended to be effective, if at all, when the considerations governing the view of the foreign government in question—the pros and cons, let us say, of the policy or *démarche* in question—are more or less balanced and the advantages of a step injurious to Israel are not perceived as strikingly greater and weightier than the disadvantages of abstention from it. Or, to make much the same

54

point in sharper terms, where the sources of pro-Israel influence are domestic, there it is likely to play a role only where a substantial measure of uncertainty colors the foreign policy decisionmaking process. Where, on the contrary, foreign policy has been firmly set, where minds are made up, where the "national interest" is virtually beyond debate, and where a particular consideration or factor—strategic or economic—is clearly dominant and informs all thinking, there no pro-Israel lobby, no matter how constituted, can ever swing things in a contrary direction. Nor, if the policy happens to be favorable to Israel, will the role of the lobby be found to have been notably significant, let alone crucial. The history of Israel's relations with the European powers great and small provides ample illustrations of this rule—that of its relations with France being perhaps the prime example. But so does the history of relations with the United States—where it is so frequently claimed that matters are otherwise. It has been thus (to cite no more than two notably severe examples) in the case of the unusually cruel American decision to impose an arms embargo when Israel, immediately upon its creation, was fighting for its life; and in the case of the absolute refusal of the United States to allow Israel to complete its military recovery in the course of the Yom Kippur War by crushing the Third Egyptian Army. At a lower (because purely diplomatic) level of severity, there may be cited the case of the extraordinary maneuvers whereby, with the enthusiastic help of the Swedish government and a handful of self-appointed American Jews, open contact between the United States and the PLO was resumed at the end of 1988. In other words, the degree of influence a pro-Israel lobby may exert is, before all else, a function of the general structure of politics—but foreign politics, rather than

55

domestic—of the country in question. It is manifestly thus in western Europe. It is thus, when all is said and done, in the United States as well.

The reasons for this curious contrast between what the conventional wisdom imputes to the American machinery of government in respect of Israel and how it operates in practice in matters of true high policy are not hard to seek. United States policy in the Middle East, as elsewhere, has long been informed by two distinct and contradictory modes of thought—and of action too. One has its expression in the classic and necessary tendency in diplomacy as such, diplomacy in all times and places, to deal with problems as and when they arise. This is the tendency to pragmatism coupled with the tendency to concentrate on matters which pertain to the short term. The other mode has its expression in a type of political thought which is in many ways distinctively American—namely, to think large rather than small and, above all, to think in terms of the *solution* of problems. This seems to follow from a deep desire (again, distinctively American) to establish an improved world order, to seek to ensure that human affairs be based on surer foundations than those that have obtained hitherto, and that men be freed finally from the endemic pain, violence, and misery to which they are subject. In the twentieth century this noble ambition has been much in evidence, from the presidency of Woodrow Wilson to that of Jimmy Carter. At a deeper level, it has been so throughout American history.

There is certainly a great deal more to be said about both modes of diplomatic and strategic thinking. The forward-looking one is, to some extent, fueled by impatience and dissatisfaction with the short-term attitude. There is something in American behavior in the international political arena which

56

suggests an enduring wish to have done with the messy world to the east, west, and south of the United States and, when all has finally been tidied up, to return home to peaceful, agreeable, inner America, there to deal at long last with the vastly more satisfying and important private and domestic matters that are central to the deepest and most urgent of American concerns. There is in the perfectly genuine American longing to improve the world in its entirety a unique mixture of idealism, moralism, belief in the uses of social engineering, self-confidence, schematic thinking, and crudeness, not to say brutality. It is all this together, of course, that makes American foreign policy, most of the time, qualitatively different from the foreign policies of other great powers: more attractive, less consistent, and, to the professionals of diplomacy, invariably disturbing. It is this too which has led the makers of American foreign policy to be eternally torn, as it seems, between the contradictory dictates of these two distinct tendencies, these two modes of thinking, on the matters which confront them: short-term and pragmatic, long-term and idealistic. For some years it was Israel's extraordinary good fortune to occupy a place at the very point at which these two lines of thought have tended to intersect.

For that is not all. Speaking very generally, what is peculiar to the diplomacy and strategy of the United States, at least since the end of the First World War, but much more clearly since the Second, is that in many regions, if not all, its purposes have been two-fold and mutually contradictory. Clearly, the United States is the *status quo* power *par excellence*. It wishes to preserve and protect, to hold together, to secure and stabilize. In this sense, its overall approach is defensive and protective. But equally, it is by conviction an *anti–status quo* power. It wishes

57

to ameliorate and to induce change. It has been very ready to foster some forces, often the weaker, at the expense of others, the stronger. It has sought to accelerate some processes (decolonization, for example), to inhibit others, and generally to encourage movement—all in the interests of an improved international order and with large, dramatic goals in mind. Inevitably, its approach to Israel specifically has been (and will no doubt long remain) variable and ambivalent. On the one hand, two generations ago the independent Jewish state-in-prospect was judged at the highest level of government to be exceedingly undesirable, if only because it was bound to upset the then *status quo* and because, once proclaimed and set up, it would constitute a factor which would plainly inhibit a swift return to the *status quo ante*. On the other hand, once established, a faltering Israel soon came to be seen as equally undesirable because of the still greater damage that its eventual collapse and failure would assuredly inflict on the new Middle Eastern *status quo*, however fragile, unstable and uncomfortable that had proved to be. Israel and the effects of its creation could not be easily undone. A defeated and destroyed Israel would throw the entire region into deeper turmoil still.

But Israel is not only an object of policy; it is a subject as well. How was and is the United States to respond to Israel's own initiatives, to its independently generated policy? Israel, like all other states, like the United States itself, has pursued different policies at different times. It, too, has veered from an effort to uphold the Middle Eastern *status quo* to an equally great effort to overthrow it. It may be argued, nonetheless, that in the very long term, it has been a prime mover for change within the area and that such change, in important respects, and on balance, has been useful to the United States. American influence in the Arab world has hinged in large part in recent years on what the Arabs correctly perceive as the American ability to prevent Israel from bringing the full resources of its military power into play. This in turn has kept open the question in what shape Israel would be militarily, and economically too, and what policy it would pursue, were it to be left without American backing. The end result in turn has been to confront the United States with a dilemma that has followed ineluctably from the contradiction between, on the one hand, America's pragmatic dislike of change and disturbance (doubled and redoubled when the source of the disturbance is Israel itself) and, on the other hand, the welcome it is inclined to offer, on other grounds, to any serious opportunity to reshuffle the political cards and deal itself and its preferred partners new and superior hands. But does—or can—Israel offer an opportunity to the United States to reshuffle the political cards? Or is it rather the case that Israel impedes all attempts to do so? In that event, the further question that arises is: How far and effectively can Israel be manipulated, or dictated and imposed upon, should the decision to attempt to do so be taken? But this is a question to which no one knows and no one can estimate the answer. No really serious attempts of this nature have ever been made—except very briefly under Secretary Marshall's leadership in the period just preceding the formal proclamation of the State of Israel in the late spring of 1948 and again under President Eisenhower in the messy aftermath of the Sinai/Suez campaign in 1956. Marshall failed; independence was proclaimed. Eisenhower succeeded, but the issue (the withdrawal from Gaza) was not considered vital to Israel; least of all had it taken on the multifaceted significance ascribed to the occupied territories today. Things have moved on, meanwhile, and the effort called for to push Israel in a direction it does not wish to go would have to be very much greater.

It might be added, parenthetically, that the most straightforward solution to the American dilemma would be the engineering of a joint superpower *diktat* for the Middle East as a whole, at the heart of which would be the repartitioning of ex-British Palestine, perhaps even ex-French Greater Syria. This could ensure something for almost everyone, the United States, the Soviet Union, Syria, the PLO, Israel—perhaps even the restoration of Lebanon in the semblance of a sovereign state. Politically, Israel would come out of such a territorial rearrangement of the ex-Ottoman Levant quite badly, unless, that is, it did not have to bear the damaging precedent of revised frontiers alone. Jordan would be worst off, however, for it would thereupon have to begin to fight for its life against a greatly strengthened and encouraged PLO. But in the most general terms, the advantages of a thorough reshaping of the states of the region would lie in the fact that all parties would be provided with an immense fig leaf (in the shape of external dictation) behind which each would have been helped to retreat to what are at present politically unacceptable, although on a realistic basis actually preferable, positions. A source of exceedingly dangerous superpower friction would have been removed. Russia and America would both be relieving themselves of the tiresome, virtually hopeless business of trying to manage relations with all the small fry of the region at one and the same time. For in practice, they would be dividing up the region into loosely defined, but easily recognized, spheres of influence. No doubt this last would be fiercely resented by many of the local Muslim leaders and their rent-a-crowd followers as a reversion to evil, imperialist practices—which, roughly speaking, is what it would be. But the sighs of relief all round might actually drown out the shrieks of outrage.

Whether the United States will actually embark on some such course is now the central question in Middle East politics. Thus far, at any rate, it has not been able to decide whether to do so. Among its difficulties and dilemmas are those which Israel's strategists and diplomats continually confront them with—in practice, of course, not necessarily explicitly or even intentionally. And what these may be boiled down to is a continual and excruciating demand for clarity. What do the Americans really wish for ultimately? Do they wish a strong Israel or a weak one? An active Israel or a passive one? Or merely a quieter life? It is many years since a clear answer was forthcoming. It is far from certain whether and when a clear answer from Washington will ever emerge.

For it is plain that, on the one hand, a firm move by the United States towards *either* target means substantial disturbance to the present delicate regional *status quo*. At the same time, and on the other hand, abstention from movement and from choice for the sake of total stability cannot fail to put an end to progress towards the solution of the fundamental problems with which the region is beset. Indeed, the American dilemma can be put in starker terms yet. It may be the case that the problems and the afflictions of the region are wholly beyond solution and relief. In that case, true American-style diplomacy is out of the question anyway. But if so pessimistic an outlook is rejected and solutions *are* to be advanced and improvements *are* to be encouraged after all, then, in practice, success is likely to be directly proportionate to the clarity and lack of ambiguity with which policy towards Israel is defined and pursued—namely, the degree to which American policy

61

is either unambiguously destructive of Israel or unambiguously sustaining. But this is precisely the decision successive American administrations have found it extremely difficult to make—not so much, be it said, because of such influence as the pro-Israel lobby has been able to exert, but because of the inherent contradiction between the two approaches which continue to inform thinking in Washington on Middle Eastern as well as on many other matters. It is not the pro-Israel or Jewish lobby in Washington that has created this contradiction. It is the contradiction which has made the functioning of such a lobby possible—and, for Israel, necessary. It is for this reason that talk in Washington of "reappraisal" or "reassessment" is always worrying in Jerusalem; and equally it is for this reason that such talk never leads to panic there, let alone premature despair. By the same token, it is the inability of the Americans to resolve their dilemmas that explains why, thus far, no true reappraisal and no entirely clear-cut and firm American policy has ever emerged.

In all this, the crucial considerations in Washington center not on American Jewry, let alone on the Jewish people as a whole, but on Israel as a political and military constituent of the Middle Eastern complex. American diplomats may worry at times about the "Jewish lobby." They may dislike it. They may try, cautiously, to undermine it. Provided they are tough-minded enough, there is nothing at all to prevent them from integrating Israel *itself* (for good or for ill) into any policy for the Middle East they may care to devise. What they cannot do, no matter what they may say privately or (upon retirement) publicly, is to integrate essentially *domestic* political concerns into a rational and consistent policy for the region.

This is another way of saying that as things stand, the communities of the Western Diaspora, and that of the United States before all others, cannot be easily manipulated by their own governments—not so long as they do not wish to be, at all events. The links between Israel and American and European Jewry cannot be made to hinge upon the will and mediation of official Washington, or Paris—unless, of course there is a huge reversal of established practice and policy on Jewish matters in the Western world. The natural path of communication and coordination (if any) is direct: New York and Paris straight through to Jerusalem. It is for the Jews of the Dispersion themselves, and themselves alone, to decide how firmly and in what circumstances they wish to maintain this path. But in this respect they are in difficulty: the political nature of the link is inescapable and undeniable.

However, something more needs to be said about the roots of the change that has overtaken modern Jewry in the wake of these and related developments, and too about the conceptual difficulties that Jews have experienced in coming to grips with it, before going on to examine its probable consequences for their future.

THREE

Politics, Divergence, and Historical Discontinuity

Writing well over fifty years ago, Arnold Toynbee said of the Jews, the Turks, and the Irish that they had this in common: they appeared to wish to alter their lot. "The Turkish legatees of the Ottoman civilization are today content—like the Zionist legatees of a fossilized Syriac civilization next door and the Irish legatees of an abortive Far Western Christian civilization across the street—to live henceforth in comfortable nonentity as a welcome escape from the no longer tolerable status of being a 'peculiar people.'"[1] Toynbee's tone is characteristically sharp, provocative, and arrogant. Like Gibbon's, the judgment is superficial, the argument skewed. Even if Toynbee were correct in his view (and I think he was not) that that was what the Zionists—along with the Kemalist Turks and the post-partition Irish—really wanted, it is plain enough that that was not what the Zionists achieved. The last thing that may be said of the Zionist enterprise is that it has achieved, or has ever been on its way to achieving, "comfortable nonentity." Nevertheless, as with the earlier grand (but greater) historian Gibbon, there is a sense in which Toynbee, in his brutal and dismissive way, did put a finger on a central feature of the modernist trend in Jewish life—of which Zionism is only one, if arguably the most important, strain. It is the desire to change course, to break the mold and, above all and in Toynbee's terms, to "escape from the no longer tolerable status of being 'a peculiar people.'"

"Escape," "no longer tolerable," "peculiar"—these are terms that strike home. They retain a resonance that antedated the events of the Second World War by several generations. They continue—in new and totally unforeseen ways—to move the minds of great numbers of Jewish men and women to this day. For what contemporary Jewish history confronts us with, always provided we examine it with care, is indeed a great discontinuity that has followed from the deliberate effort to *end* the "peculiarity" of the Jews—but a divergence, too, the one linked to and reinforcing the other. The divergence, as will be seen, is essentially between those who are wholly involved in the effort to effect a discontinuity in the course of Jewish history and those who are not and who, moreover, when all is said and done, do not wish to be. Neither the discontinuity nor the divergence are complete and clear-cut. Some may say that the success of the long effort to "normalize" even a fraction of Jewry is still in question. Some believe that it cannot succeed. Still, discontinuity and divergence in one degree or another are manifestly what the observer of contemporary Jewry cannot but encounter. It is, indeed, the central thesis of this essay that they are already exceedingly deep and are most probably irreversible.

Now, it is manifest that among the features of the history of the Jewish people in the course of their long exilic period—between, say, the second or third century C.E. and the first hesitant but real steps towards their emancipation in Europe in the eighteenth—two are salient. One is that their history is marked by the virtual absence of anything that might reasonably (I would emphasize the word "reasonably) be classed as political. Thus in the sense of high or national politics, *a fortiori* international or power politics, but also of any other type or form of politics in which autonomous power provides either the basis for action or the stake—even informally or indirectly or covertly so.

The other salient feature of pre-emancipatory times is that while it would be absurd to regard Jewry in Toynbee's simplistic and dismissive terms, namely as "fossilized" (whatever that might mean), nevertheless, in the course of this immensely long period (roughly, from the reign of the Roman Emperor Hadrian to that of the French Emperor Napoleon), it is the meagerness and excruciatingly slow pace of change in all aspects of Jewish life, not excluding the structure of relations with the surrounding societies, that is particularly striking. We should not be surprised therefore that, as we are often reminded, there is no serious writing of Jewish history to speak of after Josephus (who wrote in the first century) and before Leopold Zunz and Heinrich Graetz (who wrote in the nineteenth). It is not at all that Jewish intellectual activity in general had come to a paralytic halt. It is rather that, in the first place, change was not what Jewish scholars were interested in (for perfectly legitimate theological and philosophical reasons); and, in the second place, and perhaps decisively, that the factors which made for social change at its plainest, most rapid, and most dramatic—namely, the political—were simply not in evidence so far as the Jewish people themselves were concerned. I do not mean that Jews did not participate in politics or contribute their mite to political change in other societies and polities, or that political change in other societies did not impinge

67

upon the Jews. It did, of course, often with drastic and exceedingly painful results. But these would normally be classed by the Jews themselves as *gzeirot*—literally edicts, in practice afflictions—all essentially of an exogenous nature, the roots of which, so it was believed, and rightly so for the most part, were to be traced elsewhere than in Jewry itself. In sum, not only had Jewry largely dropped out of "history," notably out of the making of history, the Jews had dropped out of historiography too: out of the examination and consideration and, of course, the writing of history—their own history, no less than that of others, but above all, history in its classic, salient mode, the political; and within that mode, from history in those terms which deal with the really crucial and central issue, the terms which Lenin encapsulated in his famous question *Kto kovo?*

"Who whom?" was what Lenin thought most worth asking, meaning "Who will overcome whom?"[2] And it is indeed the case that so far as relations between Jews and non-Jews were concerned, this was a question that long seemed to admit of only one answer. Ostensibly, it was therefore a question there was no real need to pose. But neither was it a question there was any marked disposition to pose, even so far as the *internal* evolution of Jewry was concerned. And that is no less telling.

With the onset of the modern era, however, there has been a return to politics, and with a vengeance. It has been a reluctant return, for the most part, a slow and uncertain return at first, then one which steadily accelerated. In our own times, before our eyes, the return has become revolutionary. Who can deny that the Jews are now a political and politicized people once again, probably irreversibly so, like it or not, rather bewildered by the change, only beginning to perceive something of the far-reaching consequences for themselves (and for others too), consequences that they were and are in no position to foresee, but which many fear?

Some years ago, a scholar who has a fair claim to be considered the dean of German historians in the United States published his long-maturing account and analysis of modern Germany—roughly, from Bismarck to Hitler.[3] An odd feature of his book, considering its subject, was that its very substantial index contained no listing at all for "Jews." If you look for them in the text, however—for all that there is not a great deal about them even there—and then back again in the index, you do find them after all, indexed (and discussed) under "anti-Semitism." And so, on reflection, perhaps not really odd at all, only evidence of a somewhat old-fashioned and yet—given its inner logic—not wholly unreasonable view of the proper way to place the Jews in history, the history of the Europe of established nation-states, at all events, Germany among them. It is, of course, a view that implies a clear and particular answer to Lenin's question. Not being in a position to overcome anyone, and virtually everyone being in a position to overcome them, what kind of history *of their own* can the Jews be said to have? In any event, the point for present purposes is that the answer implied in Gordon Craig's otherwise learned and useful book, namely that the history of the Jewish people in its salient social respects cannot be other than a dependent function of the history of others, is valid no longer. It is not that Lenin's question is not worth asking with reference to the Jews. It is that now, towards the close of the twentieth century, if it can be answered at all, it is bound to elicit a much more complex answer than that which had once been customary. This is plainly the case,

69

so far as the recent and contemporary history of the Jews may be concerned, but it is so to a certain extent for all periods. There is a very strong sense in which Lenin's question has now become what is quite possibly the most instructive question to pose not only for a historian or any other observer of contemporary Jewry, but for the contemporary students of the history of the Jews in any period—to pose and to attempt seriously to answer. In the first place, it directs us to the exploration of that profound discontinuity in the history of Jewry which we are witnessing. Attending to it, the observer can hope to begin to come to grips with the nature and structure of the great upheaval. But then, as he proceeds, he may very well discover that he has something fresh to say, as much about the age before the actual onset of the change as about that which has followed. To refuse to do so is to continue to condemn himself to the treadmill of convention.

For while it is manifestly the case that the Zionist movement and the State of Israel (and all that has followed from the latter's successful establishment, along with the continuous effort by some to maintain it and by others to destroy it) are both epitomes *and* prime causes of the general development with which this essay has been concerned, it is essential to see that its roots run very much deeper. They can be traced back at least as far as the middle of the seventeenth century—which is to say two hundred years before anything remotely "Zionist" was on the scene. In the period immediately preceding the rise of Zionism in Jewry, preparing the ground for it to a certain extent, there was already in evidence what can now be seen as an initial, exceedingly cautious reversion to something approaching politics proper. True, it was anything but intentional and deliberate. Its forms and explicit purposes were almost wholly philanthropic, as befitted the stated ethos and practical purposes of the institutions which embodied it: thus in the case of the Alliance Israélite Universelle, thus in the cases of the Conjoint Foreign Committee of the Board of Deputies of British Jews and the Anglo-Jewish Association, thus too in the case of the American Jewish Committee, and so on down a familiar list. But even if the notables of Jewry who fostered and largely managed those institutions were slow to grasp the significance of their own unprecedented ability to cooperate on matters of common interest across the states and frontiers which in one way or another divided and circum-scribed them—therefore in effect, to cooperate *politically*—non-Jewish authorities, publicists, and interest groups were ready enough to note the development and, indeed, often greatly to exaggerate its significance. In 1916 a highly skilled and intelligent British minister at the Foreign Office thought fit, very privately but quite soberly and without apparent animus, to remind his colleagues of what he termed "the inter-national power of the Jews."[4] The publication a year or so later of the Balfour Declaration was nothing if not a response to a greatly inflated perception of Jewry's power and political uses. Later still, the Protocols of the Elders of Zion, fraudulent in origin, evil in intent, poisonous in effect, were likewise, in their fashion, as clear a piece of testimony to a common view as you could wish—a tiny nugget of truth being embedded, after all, in an otherwise revolting structure of absurdity, fic-tion, and nastiness.

Nothing in all this implies a picture of modern Jewry as politically united, fully purposeful, and intrinsically strong at any stage *in fact*. The first half of the present century provides more than sufficient evidence of the weakness and internal

71

divisions which have beset the Jews to their huge cost. The evidence for purposeful unity in the second half of the twentieth century is somewhat stronger; but even so it is hardly better than mixed. The question of the real nature and efficacy of such power as Jewry may have, along with the further question of Jewry's internal political structure and its capacity (and will) to wield power and sustain conflict with other peoples, is therefore of an importance that is difficult to exaggerate. It cannot—at least should not—fail to be at the top of any observer's and *a fortiori* any historian's agenda. Not only is it of immediate importance as the hundred years' war between Arabs and Jews continues to pull in ever larger numbers of peoples and institutions on either side, and as the stakes both in material and emotional terms have risen. With the return of national politics to Jewry—international politics and therefore also intranational politics—it is precisely to topics in the political life and history of the Jews that close, perhaps the closest, attention should be directed if the contemporary Jewish condition is to be properly understood. This is not because it is proposed that anything so simplistic as the Rankean rule of the *Primat der Aussenpolitik* be applied to the Jewish case *a priori*. Rather, it is because the fact that political issues are now the very issues upon which the destinies of the Jews as a people are most likely to turn can and must serve to remind us that this has always been the case in one way or another, very probably to a much greater extent than we have generally tended to believe. True, a primarily political-historical analysis of the life and history of the Jews in their exile cannot fail to appear somewhat peculiar. The effort to embark on such an enterprise would assuredly force the historian to deal

72

with questions of exceptional difficulty. The answers, however, would be of exceptional interest and importance.

Consider. The first really great question to arise in this context is: Why was this shift to politics in Jewish public life so late in developing? (Unless one wishes to turn the issue entirely upside down and ask: Why did it occur at all?) Beyond it there loom the further questions that an attempt to answer the first would surely bring in its wake. How has contemporary Jewish political behavior been influenced by the long apolitical past? When the majoritarian champions of quietism put brakes on the minoritarian champions of the shift to politics, why were these brakes so effective? And most difficult and delicate of all: Why did so many of those who claimed to lead Jewry refuse so stubbornly to respond constructively to the call for change, in spite of the evident peril in which Jewry and Judaism were placed as the twentieth century succeeded the nineteenth?

All these are issues to which the contemporary observer of Jewry is—at all events, should be—drawn. True, they have less to do with the contemporary condition of Jewry in the strict sense than with the long stretch of time that leads up to the contemporary period properly speaking. But therein lies their real importance. They have to do, that is to say, with the broad impress of modernism on the Jews and their culture, most particularly so in eastern Europe, where the greatest and most compact and most homogeneous branch of Jewry was to be found before the Second World War and where most of what was of lasting social and demographic significance for the Jewish people in the modern era occurred. It was there that the Jews as a group were still for all practical purposes one

73

of the constituent nations of the region, differing from the others—the Poles, the Russians, the Ukrainians, the Lithuanians, the Byelorussians, the Volksdeutsche, and the rest—only in two, if in themselves utterly crucial, respects. These were that they lacked the underpinning of solid territorial concentration in any single part of Europe, and, no less tellingly, were largely devoid of the political ambition to establish one. In any event, it was from eastern European Jewry that almost everything of importance in contemporary Jewry can be seen to have flowed; and it was on the quality, well-being, and, ultimately, the destruction of eastern European Jewry that almost everything hinged. By the same token, the space left by its elimination still yawns terrifying before us as we look back to discover how we came to be what and where we are. Accordingly, it follows that to examine eastern European Jewry in the light proposed here is to examine at one and the same time the sources of all that is most characteristic of Jewry at its most static and all within it that has promoted radical change.

It is essential to remember, however, that the fate of European Jewry was not decided finally by socioeconomic *forces profondes,* deep, slow-acting, as it were ecological causes, but rather by an act of explicit (and generally unanticipated) political will and as a matter of state policy—German state policy, as it happened. What is more, the ability, such as it was, of the Jews themselves to save something from the impending catastrophe and, in the aftermath, to salvage something from the wreckage owed everything to political will as well—albeit one of totally different quality, content, and ethical status. All these are further grounds for thinking that historians and other students of modern Jewry must grapple with issues of a firmly political order, and that to do so is to pose exceedingly important but ineluctable questions about the vastly longer span that led up to the modern period proper and was prior to its onset. Generally, however, these have turned out to be questions that have not much been voiced and that specialist historians of Jewry, notably Jewish historians of Jewry, have generally been reluctant to pose and seek urgently to answer.

Equally, there are here grounds for thinking that there is much truth in Benedetto Croce's celebrated dictum that "every true history is contemporary history"—which, as the relevant pages of his writings will show,[5] was intended not only to suggest a standard by which to judge historical writing, but also as a summary description of what is in the mind of the historian as he writes. The precise relevance of Croce's dictum lies in the fact that if we go along with him, there does appear to be a sense in which much of contemporary Jewish historical writing is not, or not sufficiently, "true." Certainly, this is very far from saying it is fraudulent or the product of historians who fail to cleave to the highest standard of probity. It is rather that, by and large, the results, however worthy in other respects, reflect few signs of that imaginative grasp of the past characteristic of historians intent—in Croce's terms, and in Collingwood's too[6]—on reliving it in their own minds, minds which of necessity will have been formed in, and informed by, their own, in this case *our* own, times.

That said, however, it is evident that the process is anything but simple and straightforward. On the contrary, it is fraught with ambivalence and uncertainty. It is thus in all cases. It is strikingly so in the case of the history of the Jews. For what students of history may make of the past is one thing. What those actors in history whom the historians seek to observe and account for may have made not only of their own times, but of earlier times as well—of "history," especially their history—is likely to be something else again. It follows that the historian must discover a way of maneuvering between what will turn out to be *his* initial outlook and frame of reference and those of the subjects—the historical personages—which his inquiry requires him to examine. And to understand what actually happened, he will have to accommodate the one to the other. Ultimately, all levels and frames of reference must be explicated—and reconciled—if a coherent and persuasive account is ever to emerge. The historian may figure as the director and cutting editor of the entire production, if one may so put it. He can never be the creator of the original script. Least of all can he be the author of the novel from which the script was originally derived. The history of a people, in other words, is never a matter for professional historians alone. What a people makes of its own history, and what in particular its leaders believe to have been, and actually present as, its history, are historical facts of the first importance.

In practice, some tension between the two classes or levels of reference, the one which might be called amateur, the other ostensibly professional, will generally obtain. At the amateur level there is that which fills the mind and informs the thinking of the statesman, the leader, the commander, or the ideologue, along with the relevant flock, party, cohorts, or disciples as the case may be, even an entire society or people. There are obvious and celebrated cases where a certain and very explicit set of historical opinions and perceptions seems truly and directly to have determined political thinking and action by the actors. The cases of Winston Churchill and Charles de Gaulle, along with the parties and societies they led at the height of their careers, spring immediately to mind. And even if Churchill and de Gaulle were hardly typical of modern political leaders, they are still worth recalling in the present connection because they do serve to remind us that there is no effective collective action, especially national political action, without some past— true or mythic—to rely on. Both men, it will be remembered, not only evoked the mythic past of their countries as models of immediate relevance to their own times, but believed in them heart and soul. And indeed, by no means coincidentally, they were (in the terms suggested here) amateur historians of real distinction, as their voluminous writings go to show. At the professional level, the historian of a nation's politics, the *national* historian—which is to say, the historian of some aspect of the life of the collectivity (the English and the French in these cases)—ignores Churchillian or Gaullist historiography and their analogues at his peril, whatever he may himself think of them as contributions to his art. He must seek to contend with both levels or orders of historiographic discourse in such cases: theirs and his own.

The great discontinuity in the history of the Jewish people with which this essay deals is just such a case. To begin with, there is an obvious sense in which a certain, active view of the historical past was always part and parcel of what may be termed, neutrally, the Zionist phenomenon. For it goes without saying that Zionism as a set of ideas, and the organized Zionist movement too in all its ramifications, were founded on Jewish historical memory and nourished by it from the start. The idea of a Return to Erez-Israel, the idea of engineering a revival of nationhood in the political sense, the very assumption that supracommunal organization and action were possible, legitimate, and necessary, the desire to put the relations between the Jewish people and other peoples on a fresh and

77

improved basis—these drew not only inspiration from the remembered and, it should be said, the misremembered past, but useful if admittedly ancient precedents. From those precedents (real or imaginary, it hardly mattered) there were drawn presumptions of legitimacy and rights. In a very simple and direct and often naïve sense, historical memory provided the grounds for action, for mobilization of support, for debate, and, not least, for moral sustenance in conflict and defeat. What was could be again, and rightly so. What had once been yours—autonomy, parity, self-respect, free internal development—could be yours once more. The Past, at any rate what you knew and what you made of it, was the great reservoir upon which you could draw for arguments and proofs and, above all, *alternatives* to the present.

The contrast between past and present (whence the contrast between present and future) was indeed the most powerful fuel feeding the engine of this, the modern Jewish national movement *par excellence*. In this sense, the ideological apparatus of the Zionist movement had a great deal in common with its contemporaries, the national movements of the Irish, the Poles, the Czechs, the Serbs, the Turks, and so on and so forth down the long, now more than familiar list, not forgetting the Arabs themselves, as Toynbee (and many others) pointed out. Nor should this surprise us. A usable past is essential equipment for all national movements when these are founded—and it is this that needs stressing—on revival and rehabilitation and restitution. So much so, that wherever it has proved difficult to find and resurrect one, at any rate one that is sufficiently notable, a usable past has generally had to be invented. Such seems to be the rule; and if so, Zionism and the Zionists have not been exceptions to it, for all that they had less difficulty finding appropriate precedents in their past than had most of their analogues. In their case a fully fledged national past was ready to hand. Indeed, without the rich and immense weight of the remembered and misremembered past on their minds, the purposes and actions of the Zionists in their heyday would be incomprehensible—even, it is safe to say, inconceivable.

All this is plain and evident and must be said. It must be said, too, that it is so plain and general in its reference that were it not for the curious and at the same time important ways in which the factor of historical memory impinged on the actual working and evolution of the movement in continuing practice—as opposed to merely serving as a static foundation of sorts on which it might rest—it would hardly merit close examination. In fact, the impact of historical memory upon the Zionist movement is notable in certain particularly telling, central, and operative respects.

In the first place, the appeal to the past and the very conscious, indeed often self-conscious effort to evoke it and, so far as possible, reconstitute its elements led the Zionists into a huge trap of ambivalence out of which they have never been able to escape. For the appeal to the past entailed the notions— always loosely formulated, no doubt—of historical cycle, of revolution in the strictest sense of the term, of back and forth, of up and down, of series. And, indeed, the history of the Jews taken at its most general is precisely of that pattern: in and out of the Promised Land, Reward and Punishment, Catastrophe and Reconstruction, Home and Exile. It is true that, putting aside the well-known orthodox theological objections to a Return to Erez-Israel and to a revival of a Jewish polity without benefit of divine sanction and Messianic intervention, this

79

was a pattern that could not fail to ease the path of Zionism and the Zionists to the hearts and minds of their potential constituency.

But at the same time, and much more formidably, it presented them with an immense problem in both doctrine and political practice and a towering obstacle to the ultimate capture of their constituency. For if the fundamental pattern is indeed cyclical and the cycle of Return and Exile has, as every schoolboy knows, been repeated and completed more than once, and if, in addition, the exilic periods were more extended than the others and, on balance, more significant for the formation and structure of Jewry as we know it in modern times, who then can say what is the norm? Who can say whether the Jews should see themselves rightly as children and heirs of the Davidic kingdom rather than of Babylon? And, indeed, the weight of organized opinion in Jewry, rabbinical in the first place, but lay-communal too for the most part, was for the first seventy years or so of the history of the Zionists firmly on the anti-Zionist side of the scales. And it is not clear that it has moved decisively to the other side since then. Overwhelmingly, those Jews who have been free to make a choice have voted (with their feet, at any rate) against the Zionists, preferring Babylon to Jerusalem almost as a matter of course. The consequence has been that the Zionists were faced from the first with an internal opposition not merely to their tactics, but to their very purposes—an opposition such as had no parallel in any other national movement that comes to mind with, perhaps, the sole and partial exception of the Armenian in the dying years of the Ottoman Empire.

The broad result for them was confusion of mind and uncertainty of tactic. Did one present Zionism, indeed did one conceive of Zionism, as integral and normal in the course of Jewish history or, ultimately, as a departure from it, that is to say, as revolutionary and radical and therefore, by clear implication, as hugely critical both of the mass of Jewry in its present condition and, of course, critical of its established spiritual and communal leaders as well? Did one fight on both fronts, the internal as well as the external? Or did one lower one's sights and restrict one's purposes, and maintain as low a posture as was compatible with one's rock-bottom needs and targets, to make sure that the Jews in their majority gave the movement at least passive support? In the event, and in the main, the engineers and managers of the Zionist revolution (such as it was) adopted a low posture. Moreover, they did so not only in practice, but in formal position and, if the term is appropriate, in doctrine too. They did so partly for tactical reasons, but partly, it is important to stress, because of the intractability of the fundamental conceptual and ideological issue. Did one, to take a celebrated and still lively subject of debate, condemn and deride *galut* (exile) and its adepts and denizens, to say nothing of those, notably among the orthodox, who positively cleaved to it? Or did one sympathize and tolerate or even paper over the evident chasm that separated those who had chosen Home from those who preferred Exile?

There have been views of all sorts on the subject. There have been private doctrines and attitudes, often exceedingly hostile, to *galut* and to its people: the *galutiim*. What there has never been is a clear position pronounced on behalf of the movement as a whole and followed by concrete action over an extended period. Ambivalence (as illustrated by the composition of the Jewish Agency—part Zionist, part non-Zionist, almost from the first) permeated the institutional structure of

Zionism itself. The limited, continuing, and still very real political dependence of the Zionists, at least since the First World War, on personalities and circles that are in no significant sense identified with them ideologically is now so familiar and so accepted as hardly to be worth mentioning. It turned out that to fight the anti-Zionists directly and implacably and to draw a clear, doctrinal line between the fully and even partially committed within the Zionist camp and the manifestly uncommitted would have meant a great deal more than loss of the diplomatic and financial support for which the Zionists necessarily thirsted. It would have meant the isolation of the Zionists within Jewry. It would have meant—in view of the real balance of interests and habits of mind and the true relative strengths of centrifugal as opposed to centripetal forces in modern Jewry—the risk of defeat in any struggle for the hearts and minds of the Jewish people that they might have attempted. If the fight were pushed too far and the Zionists were defeated, their claim to *represent* Jewry, to speak for it internationally and politically both more effectively and more legitimately than any other movement or tendency, would ineluctably have collapsed.

My point here is that in this struggle, the remembered historical past, except perhaps for the very remotest, the Biblical, proved to be of only limited use to Zionism. Whatever else the Jews may have retained in their memory, it has surely been the case that they recall their history as of a largely—and from the onset of the long Exile following the Bar Kochba rebellion a wholly—invertebrate people. By this I mean a people that is devoid of firm and central leadership not as a passing contingency, but for fundamental structural reasons: because it is devoid of any formal or informal means of debating national problems and making national policy. Of course, just such a structure and just such possibilities were what Zionism proposed, among other things, to provide. Equally, here were some of the reasons why Zionism was feared and, in the main, rejected. But to this condition even the Zionists themselves, notably after the death of Herzl, gradually accommodated themselves.

And yet the fact remains that Zionism did more to transform and politicize modern Jewry than any other single contemporary movement or ideological trend. No doubt its success in this respect is inexplicable except in the context of, and as an integral part of, the great sea-change that overcame virtually all of Jewry in one degree or another in the course of the last three hundred years—one that was social and cultural at its foundations even if its most dramatic and decisive consequences were political. If therefore the Zionists' failure to grapple successfully with Jewry's historical past, let alone impose a particular view of the past upon the greater part of the Jewish people, failed to undermine their own cumulative revolutionary impact upon their people, why, perhaps that is no more than one of the many ironies with which the history of the Jews is peppered.

Be that as it may, the central question we are left with seems to me to be this. The course of Jewish history has changed; that can hardly be doubted. Are the Jews then, for their part, to be so dull, so resistant mentally and intellectually to what is around them, as to fail to revise the questions they ask not only of the contemporary period itself, but of the long stretch of time which preceded it, that in which the Jewish people as we know and recognize it took on its specific shape and qualities? In sum, can good history, in this case as in so many others—"true" history, as Croce put it—fail to be revisionist?

On the whole, with some honorable, sometimes startling, but chiefly very tentative exceptions, there has been a signal failure to revise. Why this should be so I find it difficult to explain. It may be because historians and other close observers of Jewry have still not quite shaken off the habits and shackles (often wholly unconscious) of the old apologia-minded *Wissenschaft des Judentums*. Many still try rather too hard to prove (or at any rate, not to disprove) Judaism's respectability in the light of some external and artificial standard. Many are still intent upon showing that Jewry did after all progress in fairly stately fashion through the two millennia of exile, some crisis points apart and despite the attempts of vulgar outsiders to obstruct and injure it, or even bring it down totally. Above all, the once fundamental rule of Jewish public and collective life, its quietism, still seems either taken for granted and left largely unexamined, or else implicitly approved of, or (most curiously of all and in the face of abundant evidence) denied. The problem of political power—more especially the want of it, and how and in what degree that want has affected Jewry and Judaism and made them what they became—is a problem which relatively few seem willing to tackle, least of all head on. This may have had its sources in a deep-seated reluctance in all parts and classes of Jewry, by no means among professional historians alone, to touch on the ancient fundamentals of the Jewish condition lest the search and the speculation lead only to tragic and lugubrious conclusions. But now that the problems and the dilemmas of power are plainly at the very center of the life of the Jews in a wholly new and uncustomary way, and now that their public life has been altered out of all recognition, can there be any excuse or reason for failing to take a fresh, hard look not only at their present predicament, but at the long, winding path by which they arrived at it?

FOUR

The Matter of Loyalties

This is the background against which the mounting, tearing quarrel between many American and European Jews and many of those who speak for Israel—along with the dilemmas the quarrel poses for both sides—can best be seen. But the first requirement, if the quarrel is to be understood, let alone coped with, is to face it properly. For it has as much to do with the disagreeable but inescapable fact that some Jews in some parts of the Diaspora (the United States among them) are faced, however distantly, however reluctantly, with the very problem against which the old school of anti-Zionists thundered half a century ago: the problem and danger of double, or conflicting, or uncertain and ambiguous loyalties.

This, of course, is a matter of great delicacy. It is not much discussed today, which is not to say that it is not discussed—or at any rate, raised—at all. The late President Pompidou of France said fairly openly on one occasion that the Jews of France would do well to choose between France and Israel. Théo Klein, when chairman of the Representative Council of Jewish Institutions in France (the CRIF), had that very question put to him politely, but bluntly enough, more than once; and his answer is not without interest. Klein did not deny the validity of the question; but he did assert that the problem was neither very real nor very important. The Jews of France, he said, were the product of their history and that history was indeed a double one, Jewish *and* French. Furthermore, they were not the only Frenchmen who "live in such a duality." Nonetheless, reminding his questioners of the events of the Second World War in language of quite exquisite precision, he pointed out that "my personal experience in 1940 is one which has marked me. Born in France, of parents born in France, as were my grandparents, my great-grandparents, etc., raised in a family that chose to leave Alsace in 1870 so as to remain French, I realized that French society [for its part] questioned my belonging to France [*la société française mettait en cause mon appartenance à la France*]."[1]

It is true that in the English-speaking world there has always been less of a tendency to cross t's and dot i's in this regard. By and large, by a sort of mutual, silent consent, Jews have been allowed rather more room for maneuver than in lands of the Latin (notably the French "Cartesian" and Jacobin) tradition. But the issue is there nonetheless, in the wings, waiting, and in the corners of men's minds too, Jews and non-Jews. Even in the United States, where "ethnic" politics and ethnic concerns have attained a certain legitimacy, it has been brought somewhat more to the fore recently than used to be common by repeated attacks on the so-called Jewish/Israeli lobby in Washington, especially the American Israeli Public Affairs Committee (AIPAC), notably by members of the "foreign policy establishment"—some behind closed doors, some in the open—for its "corrupting" effect. Thus George Ball, a very senior member of the State Department under Presidents Kennedy and Johnson, for example: "Practically every congressman and senator says his prayers to the AIPAC lobby. Oh, they've done an enormous job of corrupting the American democratic process."[2]

Now plainly in no case can the problem of political loyalty be rendered simple, even in principle. Least of all can this be done in free and open societies where decent men and women do tend to recognize and even boldly assert a variety of at least partly contradictory obligations: to kin, to friends, to community, to private sentiment, to religion, to morality. The great question, therefore, is how the various obligations we tend to assume are to be ordered and adjusted one to the other—if they can be ordered at all—and the answer will vary with circumstances and cases and the spirit of the times. Still, national loyalty (and its consequent obligations to state, country, and legitimate government) as a matter of primary, which is not to say exclusive, obligation in all but utterly exceptional circumstances remains an accepted sociopolitical imperative in virtually all modern societies, not excluding the American.

But what constitutes exceptional circumstances? That hard question is certainly one that admits of no simple answer. Moreover, the particular matter of Jewish loyalty to Israel, or to Jewry as a whole, cannot fail to be in many ways much more complex than a straightforward conflict between obligations to country of residence and citizenship, on the one hand, and obligations (if any) to community and kin, on the other, would normally suggest. For while the obligations of one Jew to another and of one Jewish community to another—and indeed of any given Jewish community to any given individual Jew—are now only rarely held to be primary in the sense suggested here, two, certainly three, centuries ago they were indeed held to be just that. On the one hand, since the Jews were classed *a priori* as an alien people, loyalty to land and nation (as opposed, perhaps, to a form of personal loyalty to the king or lord) was not expected of them. On the other hand, as already suggested, under the principles of limited self-rule which the Jews of Europe were generally allowed to practice before their emancipation and their subjection to absolutist and centralist government, no communal offenders were dealt with more severely by and within the community itself than those who appealed to non-Jewish authorities to aid them in disputes with other Jews, let alone with properly constituted internal Jewish authority. Heinrich Graetz, in his discussion of the "state within a state" which the Jews managed to maintain in early modern Poland, most notably in the seventeenth century, reminds us that "no Jew ventured to bring an accusation against one of his race before the authorities of the country, fearing to expose himself to disgrace and contempt in public opinion, which would have embittered his life, or even entailed his death."[3] The Jew's prime loyalty (as we would now understand the term and its content) was unquestionably and well-nigh universally to his own people. This is hardly the case today.

Even if a whiff of very old-fashioned sentiment for mutual obligation and loyalty can still be detected in some Jewish circles in our own times, it is clear that its effective value is very uncertain. Recalling what intercommunal mutual support actually amounted to in the years that were hardest for Jewry in the present century, it would be idle to think otherwise. To rely upon it and on such continuing force as the ancient precedents might still be supposed to possess cannot be reckoned as anything but unwise. But greatly weakened or not—and it must be admitted that there is certainly more than one view on the subject—the problem is compounded by the unquestionably *political* (as opposed to philanthropic) quality of the kinds of mutual assistance, support, and solidarity that are now chiefly at issue.

Whenever I myself, a citizen of Israel, travel abroad I feel bound to refrain from public criticism of the government of Israel or of Israeli society—criticism with which I am very free publicly, no less than privately, on my own home ground. Even if some of my compatriots—among them many of my academic colleagues—regard this as a tiresome and old-fashioned position to adopt, it is in fact not all that uncommon, even among the very civilized and in the darkest of times, as the case of the late Raymond Aron will serve to illustrate. Aron was one of the fiercest and in many ways the most cogent of French critics of French policy in Algeria in the late 1950s. He was also—as even many of his political enemies had eventually to admit—a man of the utmost political and personal integrity. When in the summer of 1958, shortly after de Gaulle's return to power, Aron traveled to the United States to receive an honorary degree at Harvard, his hosts confidently expected him to launch a further attack on French policy. But while the change in Paris had not led him to alter his views on Algeria in any significant way, nevertheless, as he recounts in his memoirs, he decided that it would not be "proper [*convenable*] to reproduce the argument of my pamphlet [on the Algerian problem] and denounce the blindness of my compatriots before a foreign [i.e., American] audience little favorable to France."[4] His Harvard audience was surprised and disappointed. Aron, for his part, as on many other occasions in his exceedingly active academic and political life, stuck to his guns.

Be that as it may, and whatever may or may not be *convenable* where citizens of Israel are concerned, many prominent

non-Israeli Jewish personalities, even when speaking explicitly
as Jews, do very evidently regard it as their positive right and
duty to voice such criticism of the government and society of
Israel as they may have, wherever and whenever they may
wish, and in whatever terms suit them—and to do so not
merely in Israel itself on their occasional visits there (as would
be understandable and very far from improper), but on their
own home ground and before general audiences and, typically,
in the general press. Here and there, the purposes may be
partly or even preponderantly local: "The second major focus
of [the newly established left-liberal magazine] *Tikkun* was to
counter the impression that the Jewish world is simply as represented in the media—dominated by conservatives and people
who are blindly loyal to the State of Israel. We were concerned
about this because we knew that those voices were not representative of much of the Jewish world." Thus the magazine's
publisher, Nan Fink.[5] But the real thrust and purpose of most
of the criticism is of course direct, as in the remarkable yet not
untypical case of a Jewish member of the British Parliament—
an experienced politician, presumably no stranger to the most
elementary rules of political discourse across frontiers—who
some years ago went so far as to call publicly for the "removal"
of the elected government of Israel on the grounds that its
policy had "enable[d] the question of [the] national legitimacy
[of Israel] to be reopened."[6] In sum, the paradox is evident.
We in Israel (or so at least some of us think) are constrained in
our political behavior, at the margin at any rate; other Jews are
free. And the paradox is compounded by the fact that Israel,
whatever one may think of its government's policy, is an exceptionally free parliamentary democracy and its official leaders
are elected by rigorously free, open, and orderly elections.

Nothing remotely like this occurs in the Diaspora, least of all in the United States, where the national Jewish institutions are essentially oligarchic and the leaders and spokesmen for American Jewry are, when all is said and done, self-selected—which is precisely what ensures their untrammeled liberty (if they only wish to exercise it) to say whatever they think at any time and in any place.

But can those who take advantage of their freedom from restraint and quarrel publicly with their brethren be charged with *disloyalty*? And if so, disloyalty to what and to whom? What obligations (if any) do those who willingly identify themselves as Jews owe to the common interest? May anything be said to bind or limit them? What precisely is the nature of their responsibility (if any) and wherein does it lie? Can social responsibility be wholly a matter of choice? All these are hard questions. It cannot be doubted that they admit of a variety of answers. Unsurprisingly, the disposition in the Diaspora to address them frankly and openly is slight.

However, this aspect of Jewish public life, in evidence for some years, especially since the mid-seventies, would be of comparatively small import were it not for its impact (in many cases its intended impact) on real and important—and for Israel vital—political events and developments. Increasingly, the purposes of the Jewish critics of Israel (I have in mind only those who speak as Jews and claim the right and duty to do so in Jewish causes) are openly and manifestly *political*. They are out, that is to say, to deflect the government of Israel from its chosen course. In many cases, the political character of the activities in question is illustrated by the fact that they are explicitly designed as aid and succor either to oppositional but still legitimate groups and parties within Israel or, more seriously, to political organizations outside the country and intensely hostile to it. But—and here is the real crux of the matter—those concerned are entirely aware that such power and influence as they themselves possess lie specifically (but also exclusively) in their ability to demonstrate before the eyes of the relevant foreign, Western governments, the American government among them, that they, the appointed or more frequently self-appointed spokesmen for Diaspora Jewry, notably American Jewry, are increasingly disenchanted with Israel, its government, its ways, and its people. Therein lies the special force of the exercise, and that is the source of such public attention as it attracts. For it has no other. Nor do any of those concerned think otherwise. Once the lesson it purports to teach has sunk in, so its proponents argue (if not explicitly, then certainly implicitly), the American government in particular will find itself substantially freer to bring such pressure on Israel as will force the latter to change course—or face the exceedingly disagreeable economic and military consequences of America's displeasure. But, of course, even where no such explicit intention is in evidence, such is nevertheless the likely effect—to which may be added important increments of fuel to the long-standing Arab/Soviet/left-wing campaign to diminish Israel's general moral and political standing.

Neither the essential political character of these exercises in discreditation nor of course the political results that flow inevitably from them are in any way reduced by the fact that the people in question bear no personal political or material responsibility for the consequences. They themselves are likely neither to suffer nor, for that matter, to enjoy the results of their efforts in the event of their achieving part or all of their goal. They do not share the troubles, pain, or danger to which the Jews of Israel itself are liable, nor do they propose to do so. Few trouble themselves to come to Jerusalem and Tel Aviv to say whatever it is they have to say on the spot, to the people of the country and to its government directly. They tend to do no more than emerge, briefly, from their homes, offices, and studies to say their piece, or to prepare it for publication in those newspapers and journals in New York, London, and Paris to which they have regular and privileged access, and then return and go about their normal business. Yet they claim to speak from the inside, as it were; and it is their loyalty to Jewry and feeling for Judaism, no less—so they often tell us and so they seem constantly to be telling their listeners and readers—that allegedly gives them the moral license, if not duty, to do so.

Consider, for example, the terms of the continuing debate within Jewry, and within the ostensibly informed (at any rate "concerned") circles of Western society at large, on the undeniably hard, important, and wholly unfortunate question of Israeli policy in the occupied territories. It is a debate that has generally been conducted, and not unnaturally so, in tandem with the broader debate on what it has become fashionable to call the peace process. And it has turned very bitter in recent years and become a source of much anguish, indignation, and ill-feeling—in Israel itself first and foremost, as might be expected, but elsewhere in the Jewish world as well. It is a debate that is virtually devoid, as yet, of clearly defined schools of opinion—leaving aside adepts of wholly simplistic views: those who want total and immediate surrender of the territories to the PLO, as opposed to those who recommend absolute refusal to concede anything at all politically, territorially, or strategically. It is indeed a debate in which confusion of

95

mind and feelings, often very honestly admitted, is pervasive. Still, it is possible to detect a thread or two running right through much of what is asserted, at any rate in the Diaspora.

One thread may be illustrated by a report by Albert Vorspan, a distinguished member of the Jewish community in the United States. The report, which concerned a visit that Vorspan had recently made to Israel, was not particularly angry or hostile. Rather, it was an "anguished" one, as the author himself relates. "Something fundamental seems to be happening [in Israel]. The moral equation has changed. Whether we accept it or not, every night's television news confirms it: Israelis now seem the oppressors, Palestinians the victims."[7] This was a key passage in Vorspan's report and deserves scrutiny. What was it intended to signify? It seems to mean that for the author the overwhelming and overriding issue in the conflict is essentially of a moral nature, namely the issue or question: Who may it be, the Arabs or the Jews, who—in the cant phrase—hold the moral high ground? That, in the author's view, is the question that needs answering before all others. That, he believes, is the question on which ultimately all else turns.

But, of course, contrary to what it purports to be, it is exceedingly far from being a simple question. Even if it were simple, it is certainly not one that admits of a simple answer. Unpack Vorspan's succinct formulation and it is evident that its attraction for him and for others of his school lies in the fact that it does nonetheless appear to embody a general guiding principle or test which, on the face of things, *is* simple and straightforward. For what he (like many other perfectly well-meaning people) seems to be telling us is that the effective rule in any given situation, the rule by which we may be guided to judgment upon that situation, is that it is the *victims* who, by their very nature and condition, manifestly and necessarily are the ones who hold the "moral high ground." And further, that when identifying the victims, which is to say, when determining who are the genuine victims and who are not (the question on which, supposedly, everything turns), it is incumbent upon the observer to consider the *immediate* circumstances. The wider context may be set aside. The events that have led up to what is actually before our eyes or that have been reliably reported to us may be ignored. There need be no inquiry into the past record of the protagonists or their inner and unspoken motives, least of all into their long-term purposes and policies. Thus (and only thus) can the matter be kept clear and straight and, of course, moral. Thus and only thus can proper and operative distinctions be made—those distinctions upon which moral judgments pronounced at a great distance necessarily depend.

A second thread may be identified in the tangle of public avowals of deep disapproval and discomfort which have been so much in evidence in recent years. Often as well-intentioned as Vorspan's statement, always a great deal fiercer, it was epitomized by a letter from an entire group, all of whose members are connected in one way or another with a distinguished center of higher learning in the United States. Addressed to the editors of the *New York Review of Books* and duly published in its pages, it was very much the kind of protest on which that excellent journal's editors appear to put high value. The authors of the letter briefly reviewed what they judged to be the tactics pursued by the Israel Defense Forces (IDF) in their attempt to beat down the Arab rising as it stood early in 1988 and the policy of the government which defined the IDF's mission. They then went on to state their conclusion, namely

97

that "the sickening policies of the Israeli government must be labeled and attacked for what they are: terrorist oppression against an entire population. The Palestinians are the victims of a historical tragedy . . . Among the greatest of Zionist leaders were some like Martin Buber and Judah Magnes who understood that the moral purpose of Zionism could only be realized through a binational solution. But their views did not prevail, and the seeds of the present horrors were sown long ago."[8] The historical and terminological looseness in this statement—who were and who were not "great Zionist leaders," what constitutes terrorism, who proposed the binational solution, in what circumstances and why it never took off as practical policy, to say nothing of the origins and course of the conflict—is exceedingly disheartening, if only for the superficiality of judgment the authors display. Yet what is most interesting and instructive about this particular protest is that it represents a school of thought that is in one salient respect different from the first. It is not only that the tone is different. It is that whereas Vorspan's approach, so far as it can be inferred, is evidently complex, not so much hostile as pained and confused, or as he himself says, "anguished," in the second piece the violence of feeling and the fundamental hostility to Israel as constituted from its beginnings are only too evident.

However, finally, it is what the two do actually have in common that is of greatest importance. This is the belief that the crucial, if not unique, plane on which it is most appropriate to discuss questions relating to Israel is the moral one. Israel, that is to say, may *not* be treated as a real country, populated by real men and women, some good, some bad, most a bit of one and a bit of the other. It is, or at any rate it ought to be, a country of a kind as yet unknown to history—namely a stringently and exclusively moral society, one whose affairs are governed ultimately neither by need nor by circumstance, nor even the stated interests of its own inhabitants, but firmly and exclusively in the light of universal moral laws, the laws in question being those which all decent people believe applicable to their private relations. Of course, equally they are those which twenty-five centuries of Western philosophical discourse has demonstrated time without number to be exceedingly problematic, if not wholly inappropriate, when applied to the relations between polity and polity and fraught with difficulty and confusion when applied to the relations between the polity and the individual.

In any event, these are the essential terms of reference and the main framework for discussion which spokesmen for what may be termed the internal anti-Israel coalition, the regiments of letter-writers and editorialists in both the general and the Jewish press, and great numbers of well-meaning but anxiety-ridden functionaries of Jewish society, have tended strongly to adopt. Alas, these are not the terms in which the exceedingly serious and excruciatingly difficult political and strategic matters in question can be usefully addressed. There are no states, nations, and societies anywhere in the real world, least of all in the particular part of the real world in which Israel happens to be placed, which actually govern their affairs in the light of a private morality such as these people tend to rely on or even adumbrate. Accordingly, to demand of a particular state, but certainly of Israel, that it, in isolation, shall follow such a course is to propose for it nothing less than a sentence of political, if not biological, death. Far from being just and moral, a

99

proposal seriously to found national policy on such a basis would therefore be unjust and immoral in the highest degree. But in any event, moral or immoral, it is not a sentence that is likely to be acquiesced in by the condemned society in question in the good spirit that appears to be expected of its members as they make their unique contribution to the general welfare. It is therefore silly and gratuitous, no less than futile.

FIVE

The Bifurcation of Jewry

Where is all this leading? Where is Jewry being led by the often shattering events, by the unprecedented issues and structures, by the internal contradictions and tensions—in a word, by the fundamental circumstances of contemporary Jewish life? What, it may be asked, of the future, and how may it be coped with—if indeed answers to such questions are possible? So much is in flux, so great is the possibility (I would not say, probability) of another great upheaval, so rapid is the rate at which, in Daniel Halévy's well-known phrase, history *accelerates,* that it would be excessively foolish to argue that matters are moving in some clear and particular and detectable direction. The best one can do is to try to pick out general lines along which matters may move: something of the framework within which the public life of Jewry seems likely to evolve and which seems likely to determine to a great extent the constraints within which that life seems fated to be contained.

First, there is the question of the role of Israel in Jewish life, public and private. It may be that the now rather tired formulation "the centrality of Israel" does really point to a truth of sorts. But it is a limited truth and of limited value. All that is reasonably clear is that "centrality" is not and cannot be in the nature of a guiding *principle*. Appeal to it will contribute little or nothing to the solution or easing of the intricate and delicate—and for those very reasons alone inherently unsatisfactory—relations between Israel and the Jewish Diaspora. The latter cannot and will not accept subordination to the former. The former cannot assume responsibility for the latter and for that very reason, if for no other, is incapable effectively of imposing its authority upon it. "Power sharing," of which there was much talk in the 1970s (and to which, I confess, I once enthusiastically subscribed), is plainly out of the question. For "power" turns out, on inspection, to mean different things in Israel and the Diaspora. Power, political power, is necessarily either identical with, or in some way firmly intercalated with, governmental power. And governmental power is inherently and necessarily monopolistic. Whatever may be said or done inside or outside Jewry, the government of Israel inhabits a world in which Jewish communal leaders abroad, however eminent and worthy and influential and representative they may be, simply have no part. This has not prevented some members of the Jewish plutocracy from trying quite hard to *influence* Israeli policy, and so, on a *de facto* basis, playing a political role after all (even a role in Israel's domestic affairs).[1] Those who have done so have thus sought to share power after all, even if they have continued to shy away, ultimately, from responsibility. Further, as I have tried to stress, the citizens of Israel are bound (within the familiar and conventional limits of a free democracy) to obey their leaders—like them or not. The Jews of the Diaspora, in contrast, in the Jewish context of their lives, are all free at any time to go their own private, individual ways; they need pay no attention whatsoever to *their* leaders (let alone those of Israel) if they choose

102

not to do so. What is more, the leaders of the contemporary Dispersion are as free or almost as free of the constraints of political and social obligation as are their followers. The penalties for failure in Diaspora public life, indeed the very question of what constitutes failure, are exceedingly obscure. In contrast, the penalties for political failure in Israel are analogous to those which obtain in like regimes, namely one or more of the following: forced resignation, outright dismissal, political disgrace, social isolation, loss of perquisites. The examples of Weizmann, Ben Gurion, Sharett, Levi Eshkol, Golda Meir, Yitzhak Rabin, and Menahem Begin—which is to say, virtually every major figure in the country's history in turn, each and every one having suffered a crushing downfall—provide ample evidence of the speed and ferocity with which these penalties are liable to be inflicted on the very greatest in the land. In a word, there is no symmetry here, not even the illusion of one. There are two worlds, one of power, the other of powerlessness—or, at best, of a sort of pseudo-power, of a measure of influence on those individuals who do actually possess power. Accordingly, there can be no *sharing* between the two worlds' respective spokesmen and representatives—not, at all events, without a radical change of role and functions on one side or the other, or more likely both—any more than the rich and poor can share without the poor being enriched or the rich impoverished.

The second issue, perhaps the greater of the two, is what the Jews of the Diaspora are finally to make of the new world in which they now find themselves: post-emancipation, post-Holocaust, post-1948.

Here the distinction that one must begin by drawing is between the Jewish communities of Europe and those of the

103

United States. And in this regard it must be said that there are communities in contemporary Europe which can only strike one with dismay. How *can* there be an organized Jewish community in Germany in our time? Or in Austria? There are aspects of the modern history of France too which prompt one to ask whether the Jews, of all peoples, have not lost their historical memory and much else besides. But moving on from that infinitely delicate subject (upon which anyone who has been spared the horrors of wartime Europe is badly placed to judge others), there is the circumstance that European Jewry lives, but does not seem really to prosper. The major communities in central and eastern Europe are gone, of course, and are now no more than subjects for academic research, much too much of it vitiated by nostalgia and vulgar sentimentality. To the west, in Britain and France, there are large numbers of Jews, greater numbers than before the war, chiefly middle class in socioeconomic makeup, thriving economically to be sure and making a more substantial contribution to the wider worlds of commerce and industry, the professions and the universities, the arts and journalism, and general politics too than ever before. But as communities of Jews, as branches of the Jewish people or nation, they are—perhaps by reason of the very success of their members in their private endeavors—ever weaker, ever more diluted. Certainly, there is a residual loyalty or attachment of sorts. Certainly there is a tendency to rally round when some particularly painful question or problem is raised or some notably horrific incident affecting Jews as Jews occurs. But these are Jewries which manage to do no more than persist. They are not Jewries whose institutions, whose inner cultural life, and whose very future in these countries are matters of central concern to more than a tiny (if exceedingly worthy) minority of those within them who define themselves as Jews or who are so defined by others. The outer, non-Jewish world not only beckons; it dominates their lives. In contrast, the inner, Jewish world, if it is indeed a "world" in the socio-cultural sense at all, is no more than a marginal and part-time affair. And not only marginal for the Jews of Britain and France and of the smaller western European communities themselves: marginal within the Jewish world as a whole, a world that is now provided, as it has only rarely been provided before, with a focus (a more appropriate term than "center") which is manifestly elsewhere.

In part, the reasons for the endemic weakness of the communities of contemporary Europe seem to be no more than material and quantitative. It may well be that communities of thousands, even of some hundreds of thousands, that are embedded within much larger societies are now simply too small to sustain full societies of thinking and creative people of distinctive (and necessarily alien) culture, along with the schools and the journals, the clubs and the quasi-political parties, the literature and the art to which a truly thriving, promising, forward-looking national-cultural existence could be expected to give rise. There are several excellent and worthy centers of Jewish study in western Europe. There are some fine scholars. There are public institutions of high reputation and great dignity. There are individual enthusiasts. But the overall picture cannot fail to strike the observant visitor as gray. The rate of intermarriage, as everyone knows, is high and rising. The loss of Hebrew, Yiddish, and Ladino is almost—fortunately, not quite—universal. There is a strong spirit of defensiveness abroad, partly for reasons connected with Israel, but partly too for what appear to be local reasons: a defensive

105

posture in the moral and intellectual sense, but also in the material. It is a shock, and a hugely ironic shock at that, to see Jews worship and Jewish children go to school under the protection of the French police, to note that Jewish institutions in Paris, even the most venerable, carry no nameplates on their doors to identify them, to see the Paris memorial to Jewish martyrs of the Second World War guarded night and day lest it be defaced. Matters are not much better in Italy.

Do the Jews of Europe now constitute a special, protected category once again, as in the age before the Emancipation? The problem of the way in which Jews may enter into membership of the nations in whose midst they live, which is to say, the question of the precise terms upon which they may do so, the conditions which they must accept, the degree of success at this endeavor that they are likely to achieve, and the inner meaning of such success—these ancient problems plainly persist and continue to trouble Jews and non-Jews alike.

The Jew is born a Jew by virtue of the fact that that is what his parents were, but is free to choose whether to remain one or not. Does his freedom differ in character from that of the French Catholic or Protestant? The answer is an awkward one. In our secularized societies at least, the State wishes to take its distance from all churches. A priest who has turned layman and tossed his cassock into the bushes, becomes a citizen like all others, although in some cases not without suffering ostracism by the members of the community from which he has withdrawn. As for nationality, a Frenchman may change it without too much difficulty by emigrating to a country that will more or less freely grant him another. The de-Judaized Jew who rejects all ties with other Jews denies no part of his inner self; he rejects neither his language, nor his morality, nor his way of

life; for all these come to him from what we call his environ-
ment, the country in which he lives and the State which he
obeys. Yet he remains a Jew in the eyes of the others.

Thus Raymond Aron, once again, a Frenchman of the
utmost distinction and probity and, it is fair to say, the very
model of the profoundly assimilated and acculturated Jew, in
the chapter of his memoirs published shortly before his death
in October 1983 which he devotes to the—and with great
candor to *his*—Jewish problem.[2]

In any event, to a traveler like myself, the Jewries of Europe
cannot fail to seem subject to steady erosion, if not decay. They
are too small to be culturally self-sustaining. They are too scattered. Too many of their brightest and best members depart.
They are subject to too many pressures and doubts. And only
the firmly orthodox among them manage at least partly to
resist the magnetic draw of the society that surrounds them. It
may well be idle to speculate how far and for how long religion, notably religion in its orthodox version, may prove compatible with, and resistant to, secular modernity. All that can
be said with some confidence is that a form of reentry into the
ghetto, albeit a voluntary and, as it were, glass-walled ghetto,
would appear to be necessary if a reversal of the dominant secularist trend were to be engineered. But that is unlikely to be a
viable or acceptable program for more than a small and eccentric minority of those concerned. Meanwhile, the majoritarian
secularist trend in what remains of European Jewry continues
to suffer (not, it seems, unwillingly) a cultural vulnerability
that is more than likely, ultimately, to prove fatal to it.

Without a doubt, the decline of European Jewry is one of
the great, sad chapters in the history of the Jewish people. It

is all the sadder for the evident circumstance that it is not in
Europe at all, but in the United States, plainly, that the destinies of the contemporary Jewish Diaspora now seem fated
to be played out. And in the United States, as is abundantly
evident, virtually all things are different, or at any rate appear
to be so. To begin with, it is harder, or even downright inaccu-
rate, to speak of a "community": there are no central, all-
embracing Jewish institutions in the United States, no chief
rabbis, no Central Consistory, no Board of Deputies, no generally accepted spokesman for all. There is instead a large and
somewhat ragged crowd of organizations and societies and
institutions. Some are in direct competition with others. Some
are now in what appears to be their dotage and decline. Some
are still in vigorous middle age. Some are young, promising,
and full of energy. But there is among them no structure of
relative authority or status, or even a generally recognized
primus inter pares. What obtains is a free and highly competi-
tive market, so to speak, one in which the institutions of Jewry
continually compete for members, for funds, for prestige, and
for the ears of the authorities. And yet, that said, it must certainly be conceded that the components of the "market" are
(for the most part) vastly more varied, more tolerant, more
energetic, less predictable, and more imaginative than any of
their analogues in Europe. Of course, the American Diaspora
is unique both actually and historically—not least inasmuch as
the term "diaspora" is one that it tends strongly to reject. It
is very large. Its people are extraordinarily well placed economically, if somewhat less so culturally. It is remarkably free.
It is, indeed, the only case in recent times of a Jewish collectivity that is in true (if far from complete) symbiosis with the
other ethnic and religious groups and categories that inhabit

the country. But then the United States never was and probably never will be a nation-state on the European model. It is a country of immigrants, ever more so. It has the makings of a society in which sheer variety of religious, ethnic, and historical background is of its essence (so much so today that it must now be asked whether it is not even on the way to becoming a multilingual society as well). It is surely this which has made it possible for American Jewry to thrive.

Meanwhile, the forces of assimilation, the loss of parent culture and language, and the accelerating rate of intermarriage are all very powerfully in evidence. So is the powerful undercurrent of sentiment among American Jews that the move from old world Jewry and its Judaism to indeterminate, English-speaking Americanism has been a move from an unpromising past to a promising future—in effect, "progress." "You must understand," a distinguished and refreshingly plain-spoken professor of economics at one of the great midwestern state universities told me some years ago, "a move to Israel or to any other wholly Jewish society would be a move back to Maxwell Street." He was a native of Chicago. Maxwell Street was once the heart of immigrant Jewish Chicago, its Whitechapel, its Lower East Side, its Hester Street.

Be that as it may, the number of identifiable, let alone self-identifying, Jews in America is declining and scattering. With the loss of numbers and the move of those who remain in the communities away from the big cities into the suburbs and into states where Jews have been comparatively scarce, there may occur, so we are often warned, a substantial loss of political influence. There is some active resistance to this. The number of Jewish journals is still large; and they are chiefly in English (a matter of the most profound significance in itself); but what is especially interesting is that the most prestigious of them all, *Commentary*, devotes most of its thought and space to questions of general (that is, non-Jewish) interest and importance. Which is to say that the full picture is mixed. Jewish literature, history, and sociology do attract some of the young, are taught and studied in the universities as never before, and, it is fair to say, have become respectable academically. There is in the United States the one concentration of Jewish scholarship that can go some way towards competing in numbers and quality with that which is to be found in Israel. Some of its product is distinctly better and in many cases more intriguing and stimulating than anything emerging from Israel, where learning may tend to be somewhat deeper and more meticulous, but is distinctly cautious and, as often as not, dull. But much of what is produced in the United States is offered in English, naturally enough, for a readership that knows no other language, and not infrequently by scholars who seem to know no other language either. There is much superficiality. There is a distinct air (and danger) of faddishness about the entire enterprise, insofar as it amounts to a drawing back to the origins, the roots, the Tradition, and the rest through and in the universities. Will it last? one is bound to ask. Will it leave a deposit? If so, upon whom, and of what nature? These are very real questions. We do not and cannot know the answers; but some skepticism about the enterprise is surely called for.

Thus, at bottom, despite their very different circumstances, American Jews face much the same dilemmas and questions as their European cousins. Can there really be developed by them and among them a secular, indigenous (i.e., English-) language variety or version of Jewish life—I hesitate to use the term "Judaism"—which is neither founded solidly on the religious tradition nor a mere (necessarily pale) imitation of life, cultural life at all events, in Hebrew-speaking Israel? Israel itself, so we are told by the best authorities on the sociology of American Jews, is now, in this irreligious age, a central component of the "civil religion" of American Jewry. Israel is the magnetic pole whose lines of force are crucial to the ability of the Jews to orient themselves. But how will Israel really serve American Jewry? And can it continue to perform this role? Israel is no Vatican City; Israel's machinery of government is no Curia; its ambassadors are not Papal nuncios, let alone legates. Nor is Israel (in the normal American sense of the term) an "old country." For most American Jews the "old country," if it exists in their minds at all, is likely to be Russia or Poland or Romania. Nor is Israel what it originally appeared to be in many Jewish-American eyes: a sort of mendicant community, an object of (tax-deductible) charity, and therefore first and foremost a moral crutch for those who were prepared to contribute of their wealth to it. Doubtless, it may still be that in some eyes. But as more and more American Jews have begun to realize, it is before all else an arena—very possibly *the* arena—in which the fate of all Jews and all Jewries, including their own, is most likely, ultimately, to be determined. For that reason; and for reasons which have much to do with the very much less than impressive conduct of their own leaders during the Second World War; and because it cannot but seem to them that the two great contemporary communities of Jews, the Israeli and the American, must arrive at some sort of a *modus vivendi;* and finally because of the tremendous political and strategic involvement of their own government in the affairs of the Middle East and of Israel in particular—for all these reasons, then, Israel has taken on far

111

greater and more immediate importance for them than anything ever envisaged (even by the likes of Abba Hillel Silver)
upon its establishment a little over forty years ago. It has
become a source of pride, a source of anxiety, and an object
of scrutiny too in ways and to a degree that I do not think
have ever been paralleled in Europe. Indeed, I can think of no
precedent for such a relationship, namely for one Jewish community to be so involved in—or, as some would certainly say,
to be put at such moral and political risk by—another.

How matters will evolve when the American government
once again changes tack, as it is bound to do and already
(1990) shows some faint signs of doing, no one can say. Will
American Jews seek to disengage from Israel? And what would
be the costs to them (over and above the costs to Israel) if they
sought to do so? Is American Jewry as a whole built to sustain
such radical change? Can its leaders devise an alternative ethos?
Would they in such a contingency seek actively to intervene
much more forcefully than they have done hitherto in Israeli
political decisionmaking and so precipitate a truly irreversible
change both in their own status in the United States and in the
current norms of Jewish public life worldwide? On such questions as these, one can only speculate. But they are real questions and it is by no means beyond belief that before long they
may require serious answers.

The sum of all this is that Jewry, both in Europe and the
United States (and conceivably in Latin America too), has
been both united and divided by Israel, safeguarded and endan-
gered by it, consoled and disturbed, provided with a focus of
belief and a criterion of identity, but also with an *alternative,*
with competing standards by which some (a minority) of its
members will prefer to abide, but which at least raises critical

112

questions about the norms and ethos of the Diaspora in the minds of many more. There is thus a sense in which Israel, by its very existence, not only casts a shadow upon the Diaspora, but tends to undermine it. The more conscious Diaspora Jews are of their special identity and ancestral roots and the more highly they value them, the more powerfully Israel saps at the foundations of their communities. This should not surprise us. Zionism, which sought to change the course of Jewish history, has done just that. The provision of an alternative Jewish way of life, *national* life in most of the important senses of that slippery term, has been one of the greatest of the consequences of the revolution it has wrought.

Needless to say, there is a great deal more to the ever sadder story of the widening gap between the Jewries of Israel and the Diaspora. There are differences and incompatibilities which, while seemingly less urgent and less sharp, are nonetheless profound. There is, for one thing, the problem of "church and state" as it applies to modern Jewry which independent Israel, alas, is a long way away from solving—above all because it has failed thus far to determine the role of religion in politics (and of politics in religion) in a manner acceptable both to good sense and to most of those concerned. It may be that the problem will prove insoluble. Certainly, if religious orthodoxy fails to find a way—*or see the need*—to make its contribution to a *modus vivendi,* and therefore to social peace, between the state it never wanted and the state in which and with which it is nevertheless bound to function, the auguries will be very bad. Meanwhile, the argument within orthodoxy, and on its periphery, as well as among those who remain outside both the borders and the authority of Israel, will continue to resonate.

113

At the same time, it is worth bearing in mind that this is a conflict that has everything to do with the fact that, with all its faults (which are in no way greater than, or more numerous than, those that are on view in any modern "western" society), Israeli society does offer a complete, or as one might say, integrated alternative to the traditional, religiously based Jewish way of life: Jewish, yet secular. Jewish because it draws so much of its strength from the deep sense in which all Israelis feel part of, and active participants in, the course of Jewish history. Jewish because Palestine/Erez-Israel is quite simply the one parcel of territory on earth which Jews *qua* Jews can call their own with a degree of moral and historical confidence that simply cannot be summoned up anywhere else. Jewish, finally, because their culture and, most strikingly of all, their language is theirs in a sense that no other can be: it is neither shared with any other people, nor borrowed from any. Of course, all this was precisely what the exceedingly astute orthodox opponents of Zionism feared from the first, and was the possibility against which they railed two and three and four generations ago. Whereas other movements for religious change in Jewry, such as the reformist and the conservative, are and must be variations on, adaptations of, or, as some have it, dilutions of orthodox religion, Zionism—today Israel—entails a tremendous, radical alternative: Jewish life and culture refounded on fundamentally secular terms. This is an alternative which is not available in the contemporary Diaspora.[3] On the evidence, it is hard even to imagine how, even with the most thoroughgoing of intentions, a secular Jewish culture could ever be more than a sort of pale, inherently unsuccessful reflection of life in Israel—the genuine article—or, what many would take to be worse, a sort of infinitely prolonged but absurd (because unnecessary and voluntary) exile, ultimately empty and doomed to evaporation, given that the obstacles to a Return to the homeland are now purely private and individual.

But all this only goes further to demonstrate that the nub of the matter is that the gulf between the Jewries is far from being no more than a function of admitted differences over particular social issues. It arises quite naturally and inevitably as a consequence of the great, central political fact of contemporary Jewish life. This is that there are now, as there had not been for twenty centuries, two classes of communities or collectivities in the Jewish world. One class is composed of the communities of the Diaspora as we know them and as we have known them for centuries, each distinct in one way or another, but all with this in common: that fundamentally, and with very rare exceptions (such as under Nazi-German rule), they are voluntary societies, in the sense that whoever wishes to pay the cost (a largely moral cost, and one which is falling all the time) is free to leave; and that their members are subject to a sovereign power which is not and cannot be in any significant sense Jewish. The other class is a class of one, the community of Israel. Israel's Jewish citizens (and non-Jewish citizens too, for that matter, and with other consequences) are governed by an authority which is Jewish in much the same sense that the government of France is French. In brief, some Jews are governed by Jews, by their own people or kind. Most are not. On the one hand, you have in the Jewish world a congeries of voluntary societies. On the other, you have government in the full sense, with all the accoutrements of formal sovereignty: police, taxation power, diplomatic representation, armed forces, and the rest. And this absolutely crucial difference is being reinforced and intensified over and over

115

again through the years by differences of language, of culture, of aspirations, of social outlook, and above all by situation—and therefore, necessarily, by differences of interest too. All these are grounds for judging the greatest consequence of the revolution Zionism wrought upon the Jews to have been their remaking—a large segment of them, at all events—into a political nation: a subject of history, as has been said, rather than an object.

It was once argued that the social and cultural modernization of Jewry could be achieved without political aims being sought and attained. Even some Zionists, "cultural" and "spiritual" Zionists as they called themselves, preferred things so. That is now so much water under the bridge. The dire circumstances of Jewry in the course of the twentieth century diminished both the feasibility and the value of all other prescriptions for national survival. The "political" school ended by prevailing. The separate development of the Jews of Israel and their ever sharper differentiation from the Jews of other countries are facts that have come to be woven into the social warp and political woof of contemporary Jewish life everywhere. It is only the question of how the Jews of the Diaspora are now to define themselves that remains unsettled: which is to say, not how others may define them, but how they define, or should define, themselves; and whether they are prepared to do so in terms and in language such as are commonly used and understood by all, Jews *and* non-Jews—terms such as "nation," "community," "society," "sect," and so forth, no matter how slippery or vague language of this kind proves to be. For in the final analysis, this is no more than the question whether the Jews, seen as a group, are kin to other groups or not: whether they constitute a nation in some generally excepted sense,

116

or remain wedded to such categories as "unique amalgam," which is to say, insist on being regarded, and on behaving, as a special and unique case.

The question is crucial because its immediate significance is political. Nations are generally accorded rights, territorial rights among others, which nonnational groups do not possess. (Thus, not unnaturally, it is the essence of Arab propaganda—and, be it said, of Arab belief—that the Jews are no more and no less than a religious denomination, not a nation at all.) Ultimately, of course, what matters is not what is imputed to the Jews by others, but whether or not the Jews themselves want to enter the ranks of the nations. And it is precisely here that all have been in difficulty. Upon this issue Zionists and non-Zionists (the orthodox excepted) have long been divided, no less philosophically than politically. True, not to rock the boat of Jewry too violently, even the Zionists, while they had no doubt where they themselves stood and what their own views and purposes were, have tended to shirk the question so far as all the rest of Jewry was concerned. And the somewhat ambivalent case of David Ben Gurion apart, those who have spoken for Israel since 1948 have continued to shirk it to this day. The strong tendency on all sides to pull punches in this regard has compounded the confusion, which is compounded again by the evident fact that the Israelis, taken together, do now constitute, or are well on their way to constituting, a nation in more or less the accepted, general senses of the term, while the question of the status of modern Jewry as a whole continues to be entirely open. Yet the latter question is one that will not go away, not least because Israel itself continues to contribute enormously, perhaps decisively, to its remaining on Jewry's agenda.

117

SIX

State and Nation:
The National Question

Contemporary Jewry is deeply divided, then. Is it hopelessly divided? By rights, this is a question that should be in the minds of all thoughtful people within Jewry. It should, perhaps, be in the minds of some who are outside it as well. No doubt the Jewish world was always shot through with divisions and contestation. An immense stretch of time, even geography alone—a world extending from the Yemen to Lithuania, from India to Portugal and later to Rhode Island and beyond—predicated both differences of practice and a high degree of mutual incomprehension. Still, the outer line delimiting the Jewish people and dividing them from others was always clear. Apostasy was free; but once over the line, minor exceptions apart, the apostate and everyone else knew where he and they stood and what the consequences of crossing the line were most likely to be. On the other hand, all who remained within the circle of recognizable Jewry were unmistakably bound to it and to each other not only by belief in common origins and (all things considered) by remarkably well-defined rules of personal conduct and religious observance, but by mutual obligations and loyalty.

That fundamental unity has now collapsed—done for by

the slow, fitful progress of civil emancipation initiated by the French revolutionaries just two centuries ago; by the rapid secularization of ever larger portions of each and every community; by religious reform; by the physical destruction of the greater part of traditionally, unequivocally nationally minded European Jewry at the hands of the Germans (SS, Wehrmacht, and civil administration all cooperating); by the cultural sterilization of the greater part of the remnants of that vast community by the Russian Communists; by the peculiar and unprecedented qualities of the American diaspora; by Zionism. It was done for, that is to say, by the real world as it has turned out to be and by the ever greater difficulty of perpetuating national life within the old tried and true cocoon of what was once normative Judaism.

The Jews are not the only people to have been torn apart— not to say, torn to pieces—by the implacable forces for social destruction set free in the course of these past two centuries, and by the extraordinarily seductive possibilities for both intellectual and material enrichment which, at a distance, have accompanied (without mitigating) the otherwise general ghastliness. But never before in their history, not at any rate since the long exilic night descended upon them almost two millennia ago, have matters of doctrine and belief—as opposed to more immediate circumstances—so deeply and, as it seems, so bitterly divided them.

Bitterly? I can hear the objections. But if you attend to the change of tone that has overcome public—let alone private— debate in recent years on just those questions which interest and concern contemporary Jewry *as such,* and follow the lead it offers to the sources of the ever less successfully repressed irritation with which each one of the principal schools within

120

Jewry now confronts the others, you will detect extraordinarily high charges of resentment and hostility, to say no more.

As we have seen, the central arena of debate today is at the same time its central subject: Israel. And, indeed, that the debate on the great issues of Jewish society and public policy should be fiercest *within* Israel is more than natural: it would be extraordinary were it not. Questions which in Paris and Los Angeles and Manchester may appear to be moral and theoretical in essence or inspired by no more than feelings of charity and decent fellowship cannot fail in Tel Aviv and Beersheba, let alone Jerusalem, to take on aspects signifying life and death, or at the very least evoke harsh and immediate *interest*. The public debate in Israel is therefore necessarily, but also unashamedly, political. Questions relating to the unity, quality, needs, and purposes of Jewry—all Jewry, although more especially of course as such questions may be related to that part of Jewry that is bound up directly with the fortunes of the State of Israel—are matters on which all perceive that a very great deal depends: not merely personal security and welfare, or reputation, or that ill-defined state of mind that accords (especially in America) with the need to be "comfortable."

The plainly, sometimes outrageously *political* flavor of debate on the central questions of modern Jewry as it is conducted within Israel owes much, of course, to the relative clarity, if not simplicity, with which these matters tend to be viewed by the local public and the ways in which in Israel, a sovereign state, but equally a free and open society, the outcome is judged likely to affect every man, woman, and child in the country like it or not. The matters that take this flavor and shape range all the way from what elsewhere might seem so relatively marginal a topic as that of, say, court-determined alimony (the question there being which court is to determine it, which is to be the supreme: the rabbinical or the secular) to the manifestly central topic of the propriety of holding onto— or abandoning—Jewry's ancestral sites in Judea and Samaria (the question there being what policy to pursue in regard to the occupied territories). But it is as well to stress once again, that the leaders of what can be termed the Jewish community in Israel constitute, uniquely in Jewry, a "political class" in the full, Western, democratic-parliamentary sense of the term. They are, that is to say, elected officials or at the very least the legitimate appointees of elected officials. They are, in the full technical-constitutional sense, *responsible* to the Knesset and the electorate. They claim explicitly, and not without reason and justice, to lead a precisely defined public or constituency—which is therefore all the freer to disown them. They may be surrounded and influenced by a penumbra of journalists, intellectuals, political allies, clients, and sundry ideological fellow-travelers. There is nevertheless a clear relation between their status, their proclaimed ideas, their capacity for decision and action, and their authority.

It needs to be stressed, once again, that little or none of this obtains in the Diaspora. There the authority of those who claim to lead the various Jewish communities is of another, more problematical kind. Their constituencies are neither susceptible of clear definition, nor open to direct interrogation as to their will and preferences. There being no sovereign, which is to say, no ultimate authority in Diaspora, there can be neither final nor compelling decision. All are free to go their own way at any time, to accept or to reject, worse still, perhaps, to ignore. There are certain well-known and easily identifiable oligarchies. There are generally recognized institutions of greater or lesser—but latterly, for the most part, fading—prestige. There are notables: rabbis, intellectuals, chairmen of this, presidents of that. There are, as there have always been in exilic Jewry, the rich—with their own well-understood, covertly admired, overtly envied, sources of power and influence. In the final analysis, and with exceedingly rare exceptions, it will be found that these are the real makers and breakers in the organized communities of the Diaspora, especially in the United States, and that the role relegated to the man and woman who are devoid of large independent means, apart from such lip service as may be paid to their intellectual or academic or even spiritual qualities and attainments, is firmly marginal. But in any event, so far as action and a common enterprise are concerned, there are only good will and decent feeling and, in truth, a remarkable, if not too frequent and never wholly reliable, feel for the urgency of things to bring all these men and women together, if it can be done at all. I say *a* common enterprise, because it is only a well-defined, well-understood, discrete cause or problem or crisis that will in fact bring them all, momentarily, together. For the rest, it is generally a matter of loose and shifting coalitions and low-level, short-term cooperation.

Israel and its Israelis thus constitute a fundamentally and qualitatively different kind of community from all the others. And, as has been immediately apparent to all who have examined relations between Israel and the Diaspora these past forty years, it is a difference that has virtually imposed a leadership role upon them. In the welter of communities, institutions, notables, and sundry bearers of influence both real and fictitious that go to make up the face that organized Diaspora Jewry generally presents to the outside observer, the organized and (at least for these purposes) fairly orderly State of Israel cannot fail to stand out as a tower of relative strength and political capability. Whence one great source of tension subsisting between them, rumblings of which are ever easier to detect.

Is it tension between center and periphery? Is it one between "Jerusalem" and "Babylon"? Or between inauthentic and authentic Jewry? Or, however distantly, between the profane and the sacred? Or the other way about? Or simply between coeval holders of the balance between tradition and modernity? There are claimants to all categories from all sides. It is perhaps as well that these are not questions that can, or ever will be, decided by vote, or by reason, or by fiat, or, worst of all, by expert and professional judgment.

For the true overarching issue in Jewish public life, *and* to a high degree in private life, is that of the nation. It is not so much the ostensibly academic—but in fact fundamental—question whether the Jews do constitute a nation. It is rather whether they wish to. That they did constitute one in the distant past is incontestable. That in the past they themselves, as well as others, had very good grounds for seeing themselves as one is equally undeniable. But whether historians and ethnologists and specialists in the history and literature of religions put their emphasis on the beliefs and ideas that bound the Jews together over many centuries or, contrariwise, on the reality of their fixed and accepted social condition through an almost equally long stretch of time is ultimately neither here nor there. The crucial facts are that that condition was transformed by emancipation, by migration, and by warfare against them and that those beliefs and ideas began, as it were, to cohabit with—and to have to compete with—others of unprecedented vigor and of explicitly revolutionary content. The vigor was the greater for the ease and speed with which these new ideas grew on the fertile ground presented by the altered conditions. All these new ideas fed on ever more profound dissatisfaction with what traditional Judaism and its protagonists had to offer and say. And this was particularly true of the two most radical and powerful of the new tendencies within them.

One broad tendency sought totally to release the Jews from what was perceived as the bondage of the past. The schools of thought and the means proposed varied greatly. They ranged from an anachronistic appeal at the doors of Christianity to be let in after all, to positing the redivision of society into economic classes as the decisive categories, thus automatically nullifying the significance of religion, ethnic origin, language, culture, and history altogether. Either way, Jewry as a visible, functioning, social collective was to vanish. The unspoken common denominator was escape.

The other major tendency was bolder. Its various schools sought to reconstitute the Jews collectively as a nation among— and, for all practical purposes and so far as possible, like—all other nations. It aimed at "modernizing" the Jews, but at minimal (which is not to say negligible) cost to their historical and cultural baggage. It aimed most especially at providing them with the instruments and symbols of power in the interests of both security and status. But above all, it aimed at equality. Its adepts believed that it was equality with others that would at long last ensure not only external dignity, but internal self-respect.

Of the first, the great multifaceted assimilatory tendency it may be said that its *cumulative* effect is probably beyond measure. All that is clear is that it was disastrous—as much for the cohesion and overall material size and strength of Jewry as for innumerable Jews as individuals. What was lost to the Jewish people in talent and morale cannot be known. The brilliant regiments of high-spirited, decent, altruistic young men and women who rallied to Marxism in the wake of the movement's own eponymous founder, only to be destroyed by it and within it, morally, intellectually, and in all too many cases physically as well, stand as a ghostly memorial to one long, sad chapter of this the saddest of centuries. Of the many others who sought to slip the leash of Judaism individually and, as often as not, surreptitiously, there is barely even a memory, let alone a memorial.

In contrast, the second, the national-political tendency, consisting of all those who wished to reconstitute Jewry, was more successful. It was never wholly synonymous with Zionism, it should be said, even if, in the end, it was the Zionists who made the running. There were Autonomists. There was ʿAm ʿOlam. There were the Territorialists. A careful search will reveal others, some more explicit in their views, some less. But all were wedded to the idea that the Jews must finally move towards membership in the comity of nations as more or less ordinary members. Of course, the enduring questions were: Was it possible? If so, on what terms? At what cost? By what strategy? And with what long-term, initially unperceived results? For some the very act of asking such questions was tantamount to casting doubt on or even rejecting the underlying purposes of national renewal and rehabilitation. For others, asking them was tantamount to betrayal. Some sought at all costs to synthesize the new ideas with bits and pieces of ideas and purposes derived from quite different, even contradictory sources: orthodox Judaism, Marxism, Americanism.

126

None of the attempts at syncretism was ever fully persuasive. None stood the test of time, meaning that none remained impervious to attempts to modify them, often out of all recognition. Yet none are quite dead even today, any more than any of the other doctrines and formulas are now dead and without adepts of some kind, somewhere. The offerings in the great supply-house of Jewish ideologies are as varied and numerous in our times as ever. And if some may think that this abundance demonstrates richness of mind and no little inner strength, others may think it is no more than evidence of weakness of mind and infirmity of purpose. Either way, however, it does at least tell us that these are exceedingly difficult matters to which a large variety of entirely serious people have given thought, some of it commendably systematic if, on the evidence, less than fully persuasive.

In any event, its multiple variations apart, the great question in and for contemporary Jewry is indeed the national question. It is in two parts. It is the question, that is to say, whether *in practice* Jews in our own times can and do function collectively as a more or less coherent group. Equally, it is the question whether that is what *in principle* they (and perhaps others) believe it to be appropriate for them to do.

Now, these were not questions one needed to ask—at all events, these were not questions that were in fact much asked—in earlier times. It was characteristic of pre-emancipatory Jewry, for example, that expulsion from a country or a city in which they had been settled for centuries was rarely contested on the basis that the Jews had *rights* of settlement that were in no significant way inferior to those of other inhabitants. For they regarded themselves much as others regarded them—namely as aliens, as exiles from some other place, for whom

127

residence in England or France or one of the German states or cities (or even Spain, though there matters were somewhat different) was a concession and a convenience granted them on a basis of the rulers' benevolence or material self-interest—and therefore, as is in the nature of such things, always liable to be withdrawn. That being the case, the only effective way of contesting an edict of expulsion was by demonstrating that it was contrary to the self-interest of the ruler or his subjects or both, not that it was inherently illegitimate.

All that has long since changed. The admittance of Jews to general, civil society—however grudging, however narrowly conceived, even when retracted—established a wholly new principle: membership in (as opposed to mere subjection to) another national group. Membership as a matter of right and law, that is to say, not out of charity or good feeling or indifference. But in all such cases it was also necessarily membership in a group from which previously they, the Jews, had been excluded; and, what is a great deal more important and telling, into which previously they themselves had never seriously sought entry. Moreover, it was necessarily membership in a nation with another history and another tradition—often one of direct conflict with the Jews themselves—and with other, very different, initially incomprehensible symbols and sources of group loyalty, with another language, another culture, another literature, and, of course, another religion.

How far could traditional Judaism and traditional collective *and* private behavior be rendered compatible with such membership in a wholly new group—even half-hearted, even tenuous membership—especially when it, the group into which the Jews wished, or were invited, to be absorbed, was itself culturally and politically self-conscious and well defined? Here

128

was a question with which all Jews in modern times have had to wrestle in one way or another. Here were the makings of a condition of social and psychological uncertainty in which all but the most obtuse of modern Jews have been liable at one stage or another of their lives to see themselves entrapped. Here, of course, were the sources of the urge to break free from what some felt had become an intolerable dilemma.

The history of the national question in modern Jewry is not yet over. Needless to say, it has yet to be written. It is perhaps not unreasonable to suspect that it will never be written: it would have to embrace too many communities, too many ideas, too many barely related social and political events and developments, too many societies and states in which Jews have happened to be embedded and in which, and with whom, they have had to try to make their peace and seek accommodation. The history of the Jews can never be conveniently circumscribed, let alone rendered hermetic: the history of the Jews in their dispersion must always be in some degree a history of non-Jews as well.

It is very precisely for this last reason that the regaining of political rights and capabilities over Erez-Israel/Palestine eighteen centuries after the last vestiges of Jewish autonomy had been obliterated by the Romans must be reckoned a stunning achievement. In particular, the success of the Zionists in winning through to their goal must be measured against their own small numbers and absurdly limited resources and the vast forces marshaled against them: Britain, still the preponderant power in the Middle East, her Arab allies and satellites, and, for much of the crucial period, although never with absolute consistency, the United States as well.

Opposition to the Jewish cause had many sources, some atavistic and ugly, some heartless, and some—given the terms in which statesmen tend to conceive their function—ostensibly rational and respectable, even, in their way, well-meaning. They could be all these things at one and the same time.[1] But the nub of the matter, at all levels and for all concerned, was the idea of there being a Jewish state at all. To some it seemed an enterprise that was inherently incredible, if not perverse. Some thought it fraught with incalculable and unspeakable dangers. Some judged it (as some still judge it) contrary to the fundamental teachings of religion—all three monotheistic religions, as it happens: Muslim, Christian, and Jewish. Whatever the argument, its enemies accounted it (and many still account it) a project to be fought hard and with every available political and military weapon. In 1948, with so much hostile force arrayed against them, with the U.S. secretary of state's harsh warnings not to proceed with the proclamation of an independent state ringing in their ears, not all the members of the inner Zionist leadership itself were inclined to support wholeheartedly so momentous and irreversible a decision. Nevertheless, in the end, it was precisely with a genuine sense of historical responsibility and the belief that May 15, 1948, presented an opportunity that might never be repeated that, led by a few bold spirits, they were impelled to leap into the unknown after all.

The state the Zionists built continues to bear the marks of its birth. It is an isolated state. It is in perpetual conflict with most of its neighbors. It is devoid of natural or formal allies. It is therefore forced to make the best of such cooperation as it can muster in the international arena. Some of its political and military alignments have been fleeting; some have been durable. None have been fully reliable, least of all in times of adversity, nor, as is in the nature of things political, could they have been. Israel has therefore been thrown back, as perhaps no other modern state has been, on its own intrinsic resources, one consequence being that, as from the first, it continues to rely to a high degree on the loyalty and support of Jewish communities elsewhere. In crude material terms such support cannot be (and is not) very great; nor can the loyalty be absolute; and signs of erosion of both the one and the other are, as we have seen, much in evidence. All in all, there is both more than a little truth in the view that in the Jewish state there are perpetuated some of the ancient, peculiar, and anomalous characteristics of the Jewish people, and, at one and the same time, a little less truth in that proposition than there once used to be. For the weaker the political ties binding Jews in Israel to Jews elsewhere, the less anomalous the State of Israel will seem to be, and will in fact become.

It is worth recalling that the fundamental rationale for Zionism was that the Jews cannot avoid assuming responsibility for their own lives and fortunes and are in duty bound to organize and equip themselves to discharge that responsibility to the full. This has now been realized—at all events for those Jews who have chosen to live in the Jewish state. And it is the increasingly sharp divide between those who do so choose and those who do not that informs and colors and to a large extent sets the terms of all serious public debate within contemporary Jewry.

But the deeper reasons for the fissure and for the contemporary debate conducted across it, over and above the tensions and irritation of the moment already referred to, are not hard to detect. In part, the fissure is a product of the increasingly pervasive sense that it will prove beyond the power of the State

131

and its citizens to perform that which had always been thought to be one of their primary functions. Israel serves today, as it has always served and will no doubt continue to serve, as a refuge to which all Jews may turn as of right and in which they may live as free men and women if that is their wish. Of its will and ability to do so it has offered ample—often dramatic—demonstration time and again. The door is always open: on principle, by law, and, it must be added, of necessity. But plainly, Israel is not a country that can offer the firm, safe, and protected haven its founding fathers originally had in mind. Nor is it likely to be able to do so for many years to come.

Then it must be remembered that the Zionist movement was overtaken by events. Eastern European Jewry was first reduced, for all practical purposes, by the enclosure of some three million Jews within Communist Russia; it was then subjected to the terrible war of extermination conducted against it, and against the Jews of all Europe, by the Germans during the Second World War. In direct consequence, the Jewish state came too late for all but a fraction of the very people to whom it had originally been intended to offer succor and who were most suited to it by reason of culture, by inner social cohesion, by relative absence of assimilatory tendencies, by basic political and national belief, and, above all, by need.

In contrast, the *contemporary* Diaspora consists, for the most part, of a different class of people, differently placed, whose approach to the Jewish national movement necessarily starts from different premises. The Jews of North America, western Europe, South Africa, and Oceania (to whom the present remarks are limited: those of the Soviet Union and Latin America would require separate treatment) are, before all else, those who have long since had the full benefit of emancipation

132

and who therefore generally believe that it is for them as *individuals* to determine the nature and degree of their commitment to Jewish communal and *a fortiori* national concerns. Accordingly, the matter of Zionism has tended to present itself in their eyes as a free ideological question, a matter of choice rather than of necessity or duty. Thus, perhaps inevitably, it has tended to be of real and practical interest only to a very small minority among them. There is a continuing trickle of immigrants into Israel from the western countries; but, by and large, the demographic balance between the two great sectors of modern Jewry remains stable—which is no more than another way of saying that there is roughly equal movement in both directions.

What then of the quite large numbers of self-styled "committed" Zionists who nonetheless retain their residence in the Diaspora and their supreme political loyalty to the countries of their residence? The truth, surely, is that it is no longer clear what "Diaspora Zionism" can possibly consist of, now that the State exists and that its gates are open—unless it amounts to no more than generalized, pro-Israel good will. Nor is it clear how it may be distinguished from the undoubtedly warm, but low-level, undifferentiated sympathy and support for Israel that, despite all the tension and misunderstanding, is still common enough in Jewish communities almost everywhere, so long as matters do not really touch on the delicate question of explicit personal commitment.

There are many reasons why at least this general sympathy and interest should still be prevalent, even if less so than a generation ago. Chief among them, it would seem to me, are the lingering distrust that virtually all Jews retain for the non-Jewish world and the accompanying gut feeling that an attack

133

on one can facilitate, even precipitate, but most certainly signify, an attack on all. It is, of course, a form of distrust that varies enormously in intensity and quality, with time and with place, with personal experience and social standing, and with temperament. It is perhaps most explicit and least ambivalent among those who are still very closely wedded to the ancient Jewish tradition itself, which is to say among the orthodox: it is not too much to suggest that they are schooled in it. But it is there to be traced and there to be ignited—by chance events and incidents of all kinds, by any of the myriad signs and symbols that virtually all Jews, however remote they may be in their daily lives from the collective concerns of Jewry, respond to quickly enough even when they seek to reason with themselves and with others, and damp down the old, familiar onrush of anxiety, not to say fear. There must be few Jews anywhere, however ignorant they may be of Jewish public affairs, or uninterested in them, however intent upon the pursuit of immediate, personal, and worldly well-being, who have not retained somewhere in their psyche the sense that the outer world can be enormously threatening and that, ultimately, as the Irish have it, it is "ourselves alone."

Nothing has done so much to reinvigorate such a sense of threat, part real, part imagined, as the turn taken by the Arab-Israeli conflict in the course of the last dozen or so years. In part, this evidently sad (some would say anachronistic) development has had much to do with the intensification of the conflict in recent years and with Israel's manifest inability to deal with it by such sudden, quick, and (for Israel itself, but no less for Diaspora Jewry) relatively painless *coups de théâtre* as it had managed to perform in the past. But it has probably had more to do with the substantially less superficial (which is not necessarily to say really better informed) outlook on the conflict as a whole that has begun to possess many of the minds of those who see themselves as "concerned."

The roots of the long war between Israel and the Arab states and the Palestinian Arabs have always lain in the plainly incompatible purposes and interests of the Jewish and Arab national movements as they have come to be formulated and reformulated in the course of the past one hundred years or so, but most particularly since—and to no small degree because of—the collapse of the Ottoman Empire. No reasonable person would want wholly to dismiss the possibility, let alone the hope, that ultimately those conflicting purposes will have been rendered more or less compatible by the eroding effects of time, experience, and the advent of new concerns, or new threats, the nature of which none can yet envisage. But for the time being, and most probably for many years to come, the war—cold at times, hot at others—will most probably persist, neither side as yet evincing really serious evidence of infirmity of will to pursue it. Thus, the effects of this protracted war on the cohesion and morale of Jewry as a whole, but more specifically on the relations between Israel and the Jewish Diaspora, seem likely to deepen. Once again, it is no exaggeration to say that the affairs of Israel in all their ramifications are now the central issue in Jewish public affairs worldwide.

One reason for this is that the conflict in the Middle East is indubitably a conflict between nations. It is so perceived by those most directly involved. In broad terms, it is so perceived by virtually everyone else. Given its costs and its dynamic, it may be said too that even if it were not, the protagonists would be impelled so to present it, the easier to call upon all those who might reasonably be claimed as kith and kin as

135

much for moral as for material and political support. And indeed, one way or another, Arabs on the one hand, Jews on the other, regardless of their own immediate interests and however remote they may be geographically from the actual scene of conflict in the eastern Mediterranean basin itself, have tended increasingly to be sucked into it. Some have joined in the fray willingly enough. Others have done so not without disquiet, reluctance, and even (at least on the Jewish side) a measure of overt protestation.

It is true that there are those who argue that, with the war between Israel and the Palestinian Arabs and the latter's allies (the Arab states) having taken on a national character, in effect Israel fights not only for itself, but for (even if not with) the Jewish people as a whole. Others resist this view, expressly because this is the claim that gives the problem of the relationship between Israel and the Diaspora its particular urgency and, as they see it, its particularly unfortunate edge. It is, of course, demonstrably the case that the greater Israel's reliance on the Diaspora, the more it necessarily involves the Diaspora in its affairs. The more it involves it in its affairs, the more it endangers it by leading it into conflicts and contestations of which otherwise the Diaspora might be free. The evidence that Israel and its affairs do tend continuously to rob Jews of the Diaspora of their long sought for and so very recently acquired peace of mind is abundant. And in such a context, what, on the face of things, would seem to be the political logic entailed by the new structure and circumstances of Jewry does turn out to be especially revealing and painful. For if the Diaspora is now to be ever more closely involved in Israel's travails and conflicts, let alone in some ways and in some degree actually to be put at risk by Israel, the stronger would seem to be the argument for its real and compelling involvement in the making of Israeli foreign and strategic policy for its own protection—whether by means of fully institutionalized and systematic coordination of approaches or through some looser, more innocuous, but still effective and regular consultation.

However, the obstacles and objections to such a course are, as I have suggested, immense. It is true that to embark upon it would begin that very clearing of the way to the founding of *all* contemporary Jewry on a coherent basis such as would accord with modern ideas about states and nations. But that is precisely the process about which modern Diaspora Jewry has tended to be most ambivalent. Clearing the way would doubtless do something to clear the air. But if some would welcome it, many more would fear it and its likely effects and resist it to the end. In the final analysis, an explicitly political tie between the various Jewish communities, one resting equally and expressly on common interests and common responsibilities, would go far finally to confirm and establish the Jewish Risorgimento as a matter for *all* Jewry, rather than a mere fraction of it. At the same time, it would serve at least partly to undo the long process of civil emancipation within the various countries of their residence that was initiated on behalf of the Jews two centuries ago and generally welcomed by them. It follows that as things now stand, this is not a purpose to which Diaspora Jews, by and large, can be expected to subscribe. And thus the tension that subsists between so many of the more reflective and articulate citizens of Israel and their analogues in the Diaspora has its roots both in certain perceived but incom-

137

patible interests and in the equally profound difference of ethos that separate them. It is very hard not to see these differences as unbridgeable.

It may be worth recalling at this point that the essence of the Jewish national revival was a change of mood. A guarded optimism replaced the old stolid fatalism—thus at least in those portions of Jewry that had been touched by modernity and felt something of its attractions. Change, movement, novelty, the future itself—all these took on a compelling attraction for the promise they were thought to hold, as values in their own right, as distinctive, necessary attributes of improvement. The past could now be eyed critically. It could even be rejected. It could be argued that the old rules of conduct need not, probably could not, obtain any longer. The options open to the individual seemed to double and redouble over and over again: new occupations, new lands of settlement, new styles of living, dress, and behavior, even of worship, new forms of social and political action—all were now available, or about to be, and in innumerable combinations one with the other. As for the traditionally minded, they, for their part, had no choice but either to accommodate themselves to the new mood or to turn in upon themselves as best they might, perhaps irrevocably, accept derision or worse at the hands of those who were, in contradistinction, drawn willingly into the world of movement, and to fight all such forces for change as they could identify—Zionists, socialists, assimilationists, Hebraists, secularists, outright religious reformers and, often no less bitterly, the moderates within their own camp—and all with whatever force and determination they could muster. In practice, their greatest effort would now be directed towards a raising of whatever drawbridges had remained to carry traffic between their own embattled fortress of traditional Judaism and the untidy, ungovernable, disgraceful world outside it. The fight would be for the soul—and, of course, the loyalty—of the commonalty, the protagonists being respectively the partisans of past verities and of future possibilities.

Needless to say, the central, critical *locus* of that fight, where both camps believed its outcome would ultimately be determined, was for a very long time in eastern Europe. It was there, as has been pointed out, that the largest and most compact of the still unassimilated portions of Jewry were to be found. These were the portions moreover that were the hardest pressed and, as we now know, but many had always suspected, in greatest danger. This great demographic reservoir was in large part the source (within a matter of two generations or so) of all the new communities and modern social types, notably those to be found in North and South America. Out of it, so the Zionists believed, would come the population of the independent Jewish state-to-be—in itself nothing if not the embodiment both of the Jewish national principle in its salient modern form as understood in eastern Europe and ostensibly the most feasible, large-scale, and radical solution to the afflictions of that Jewry.

But then, as it happened, long before the Jews, unassisted, could manage to determine their own cultural and political fate, it was settled for them. The great arena in which the fate of Jewry as a coherent nation was to have been played out was swept clear. The structure of what remained of modern Jewry was altered out of all recognition. Spokesmen for the contending schools could continue to plead for the souls of the Jews of Europe; the bodies were largely gone. The arguments and the rhetoric might be much as before; the *real* terms of the

139

problem of Jewry and Judaism in the modern world could not unreasonably be judged to have been transformed. In any event, the establishment of the new Jewish State of Israel was enough to shift the general attention elsewhere. Suddenly, painfully, the Jews—at all events some Jews—had reentered "history" after all and in classic form: as an armed power, in war, as a not inconsiderable factor in the international interplay of states. In a word, modernity had caught up with them at last and with a vengeance. Or, better still, they, at last, had caught up with it. Either way the Jews as a people were now no longer wholly eccentric and isolated, but afloat, like it or not, on virtually all the great currents of worldwide social and political movement. And so despite the disaster and the infinite pain inflicted on the collective psyche, despite interminable conflict with the Arabs and its ever higher costs, despite the tensions within Jewry itself as adjustment to the new structure limped behind evident needs, the general mood ought not to have been too dark—not at any rate for the modernists. It was not unreasonable to think that towards the end of the twentieth century, optimism would indeed be the order of the day. The worst was over. The future could not but be vastly brighter than anything still held in living memory.

In the event, today, in this last decade of this bitter century, such optimism is at a premium. The hidden flaw in the thesis that Jews owed it to themselves in the past, and owe it to themselves today, to embark unreservedly upon the enterprise of national revival has turned out to be a practical one. It lies, quite simply, in the unwillingness of so many of their numbers to do so. That much is evident—so much so that it has become not merely fashionable but to many minds eminently reasonable to argue that, barring a second great catastrophe and a drastic reversal of fortunes in the Diaspora, minds are set and matters will remain very much as they are—and for quite as far as the prophetic eye may claim to see. This is to say that no marked change can be expected to occur in the balance of opinion in Jewry on any of the matters with which this book has attempted to deal, short of change in Jewry's actual circumstances, more specifically a drastic change for the worse. But the thought that the unity and political reconstruction of the Jewish people might depend in practice on fresh misfortunes being visited upon it is not merely paradoxical but—even to the most ardent proponent of such reconstruction—intolerable.

Where then does that leave us? Surely, in the first place, with a nervous, ever more tenuous, ever less happy association between the Jews of Israel and Jews elsewhere. Secondly, with the prospect that the divergence between the two classes will continue to grow. Thirdly, in brief, with the observation that what confronts us finally is a state of affairs such that the conception, let alone the constitution, of Jewry as, effectively, a single people is ever more problematic. Thus in practice. Thus in theory. Are we then to begin to think in terms of two— or three, or even four—Jewish peoples? An absurd idea, on the face of things, certainly one that is wholly without precedent, one that runs directly and unmistakably contrary to all teaching and belief and the deepest sentiment of millions, even in our own time. Contrary to much that still guides practice, too. And yet, as I have argued, consideration of the real circumstances and of the central interests of the major Jewish communities, and of what, on the evidence, seem manifestly to be the broad lines of future development, does seem to lend greater plausibility to such an outlook than conventional thinking would ever allow.

That said, however, neither the broad national question in modern Jewry, nor the other, related issues and questions to which this essay seeks to draw attention, are matters which Israel, its people, and its government are themselves in a position to deal with. Nor would they be wise to attempt to do so. These are questions for the Jews of the Diaspora to settle. It is they who must and it is they who will determine the relationship with Israel that best suits them. It is they who must decide whether they prefer to fall back on tradition to sustain themselves culturally, or seek something fresh and of their own devising and make their best judgment whether or not it will serve them. It is they who must decide whether the great change that has overcome the Jewish world as a consequence of the establishment of a free, sovereign state governed by and for Jews is one from which they must, so to speak, insulate themselves; and whether the mixture of dissatisfaction, embarrassment, envy, outrage, admiration, misunderstanding, pity, and love with which they seem to regard Israel and the Israelis at various times and under various stimuli is not inherently intolerable and damaging to all concerned. Much hinges on their decision. For the longer this tension and this instability in the contemporary Jewish world last, the greater is the likelihood that in the end the *two* Jewish peoples—still attached, still embryonic as distinct organisms—will fly apart: one here, one there; one largely middle-class and Euro-American, scattered in ever smaller packets, highly differentiated, part-time in its Jewish involvements; the other largely proletarian and Euro-Mediterranean, relatively compact, bound together ever more strongly by language, culture, political and military institutions, and, of course, immediate circumstances. To an old-fashioned mind, the prospect of such a bifurcation is in some ways immensely disturbing. In other ways, albeit unanticipated, it may not be a wholly unsatisfactory outcome of—and a solution to—the present crisis. It will, at the very least, perform the much needed and long delayed function of concentrating minds and clearing the air.

But this is a prospect that turns on an irony. If what we are likely to witness at the turn of the century is a certain parting of the ways, with the Jews of Israel, ever more bound to each other by language, culture, needs, and political identity, pursuing a destiny of their own devising as best they may, and with the others, dispersed in several dozen states, ever more absorbed in and absorbed by the larger societies to which they belong and therefore necessarily intent on other purposes and another destiny—this will have been in no small measure the unintended consequence of the rise of the modern national movement itself. By its own achievements, by establishing a community which differs in quality and ethos from all others, it has evidently gone far already to deprive the Jewish people of one of its central myths: the myth of unity. It is true that such basis in social reality as the myth has had has long been eroding anyway. Yet it has never worn quite away. It has never been, even in the worst of times, without some foundation in fact. The very looseness of things in this realm has allowed a certain plausibility to the notion that the Jews retain substantial forms of unity even in the modern age, even when divided and redivided by language, by essential culture, by political allegiance and by vast stretches of ocean. The habits of mind in Jewry and outside it were such that it was as if, for all the world, nothing had *really* changed since pre-emancipatory times. Now, in our own time, into what was for Jews a not entirely uncomfortable or inconvenient looseness of condition, terms, and thinking, there has been injected the hard, clearly defined body of a sovereign state—with consequences that are plain to see, chief among them being an extreme confusion of mind.

That it is fruit of the national cause at its most fervent that may very well turn out to be the decisive engine of ultimate disunity in Jewry is, of course, exceedingly disconcerting even if, on reflection, it may be judged an inevitable development. For what the Zionists introduced and what Israel established in Jewry has been politics. And what divides Jewry, insofar as it may be reckoned to be divided, is, once again, before all else, politics. It is all very new. It will take much getting used to. It may even be that some of the confusion of mind will be reduced and some of the resulting dilemmas resolved. But the irony remains. And few things are as destructive of optimism as paradox and irony.

Afterword

So complex and intensely controversial a subject as that with which this essay attempts to deal puts the author before an insoluble dilemma. The sharper the argument, the greater the simplification. The greater the apparatus of supporting evidence and the more extensive the effort to preempt criticism by anticipating it in the text, the greater the danger of obscuring the points that are central to the purpose of the undertaking itself.

Let it be entirely clear, however, that this is a book about the Jewish people, not about Judaism. It is not about the religion or philosophy or culture of the Jews. Certainly, the matter with which it deals has much to do with the ideas that may be found to inform large parts of Jewry, but it is not at all about ideas in the abstract. It is about people and society. But again, not so much about individual men and women in their private lives and capacity, as about men and women *taken together* as members of a society—in fact a very particular society—and about the character and contemporary evolution of that society. It is therefore too, naturally and without apology, about that society's likely fate.

Were it not so ponderous, the book's published title, or subtitle, might well have been *Contemporary Jewry and Its National Question*. For it is indeed the *national* question in Jewry—or, as it might equally be phrased, the question (and problem) of Jewry *as a nation*—that lies at the heart of the crisis that besets the Jews today, all of them, in all communities, in one way or another, I have no hesitation in saying.

That the Jews, historically, were a "nation" in every important sense of that infinitely tricky and provocative term can hardly be gainsaid. Some historians have gone so far as to argue that it was the Jews (with the Greeks) who were the original inventors of the concept, at any rate in the Western world, apart from constituting the prototypical case of the actual phenomenon. That, of course, is not the whole of the—and their—story. That the religion and culture (high as well as low) of the Jews were intimately and inextricably bound up with their nationhood over very many centuries is beyond question. What can be seriously, if somewhat fruitlessly, debated is only the subsidiary question whether their ancient faith should be seen primarily as the instrument of their national preservation, or contrariwise, whether it is their peoplehood that should be seen as the means whereby their religion was defended and preserved, and not without success, against successive, near fatal onslaughts by pagan, Christian, and Muslim rivals.

But these matters, it is contended, have now been relegated to the shade by a larger and vastly more urgent one. It is that of the very survival of Jewry as a people at all—at any rate in anything like the form in which traditionally and historically it had functioned and in which it had most commonly been recognized by Jew and non-Jew alike. Today, at the end of the unspeakable twentieth century, it is not too much to say, that the survival of Jewry as a discrete people, its various branches

146

bound to each other by common ties of culture, responsibility, and loyalty, is entirely in doubt. It is with the reasons for such doubt and with the salient causes of the changes and contradictions which have undermined the ancient structure of Jewry in the course of these past two centuries that this book is concerned.

Inevitably, the discussion has led to the matter of the relations between Diaspora Jewry and what might be termed the Jewry of Israel. While it is right to say that the roots of the present malaise (if not disorientation) which characterizes world Jewry today do not lie exclusively in that domain, still, plainly, the rise of an independent Jewish state has both revolutionized and destabilized the Jewish world. It was inevitable, therefore, that a good part of the essay be devoted to a consideration of its consequences. But let it be clear: my purpose was not so much to bring the viability or legitimacy of the Diaspora into question as to argue that the *interests,* and therefore the underlying tendencies and viewpoints, of American and other Jewries, cannot fail to differ crucially from those of Israeli Jewry. And that is one key reason, quite conceivably the chief reason, why willy-nilly the Jewish world—beaten by assimilation on the one hand and by destruction and threats of further punishment on the other—is now coming apart. Where there was once a single, if certainly a scattered and far from monolithic people—indeed, a nation—there is now a sort of archipelago of discrete islands composed of rather shaky communities of all qualities, shapes, and sizes, in which the Island of Israel, as it were, is fated increasingly to be in a class by itself.

In sum, the old unity of Jewry, however fragile, however problematic, essentially a function of the old sense and, yes, the old reality of nationhood, lies shattered today, almost beyond repair. But my intention here has by no means been to complain about this or any other feature of Jewish life, either in the Diaspora or in Israel. It has been to explore and, if possible, account for what is now before us: the waning of the Jewish nation.

Notes · Index

Notes

1. The Plunge into Modernity

1. Cited in Robert Anchel, *Napoléon et les Juifs* (Paris, 1928), p. 16.
2. "Il existe parmi ces hommes la loi inhumaine d'opérer sangui-nairement sur l'enfant mâle qui naît, comme si la nature n'était pas parfaite. Ils portent la barbe longue par ostentation et pour singer les patriarches desquels ils n'ont pas hérité les vertus. Ils prati-quent une langue qu'ils ne connaissent pas et qui n'est plus usitée depuis longtemps. En conséquence, je requiers la commission provisoire de leur interdire ces usages et d'ordonner qu'un auto-dafé sera fait à la Vérité de tous les livres hébreux et principale-ment du Talmud dont l'auteur a été assez fripon pour leur permettre de prêter à usure aux hommes qui ne seraient pas de leur croyance." Ibid., p. 18.
3. Ritual slaughterer.
4. Ritual bath.
5. *The History of the Decline and Fall of the Roman Empire,* ch. 15.
6. "Décret impérial portant sursis à l'exécution de jugements rendus en faveur de juifs contre cultivateurs non négociants de plusieurs départements de l'empire, 30 mai 1806." In A. E. Halphen, ed., *Recueil des lois . . . concernant les Israélites* (Paris, 1851), pp. 18–19.
7. Ibid., pp. 257–258. English translation by F. D. Kirwan, in

D. Tama, ed., *Transactions of the Parisian Sanhedrin* (London, 1807), pp. 149–156 (slightly amended).

8. Quoted in James Joll, *Intellectuals in Politics* (London, 1960), p. 66.

2. The Transformation of Jewry

1. Emphasis in original, which runs as follows: "Les aspirations millénaires des Juifs, surtout des prolétaires de Pologne et de Russie, ne sont ni socialistes, comme leur situation sociale porte à en supposer, ni même nationales comme les déclarations de leurs intellectuels prétendent; elles sont essentiellement talmudiques, c'est-à-dire religieuses. Les légendes dont les misères de ces pauvres diables ont été bercés leur font entrevoir Jérusalem instauré comme le [remède] à tous leurs maux, ce sera le Paradis sur terre où le Dieu d'Israël reposera triomphant . . .

"Il ne faudrait pas [minimiser] la valeur de ces rêveries, ni les mépriser inconsidérément. Même parvenu à des hautes situations dans des pays d'égalité civile, les Juifs intelligents et instruits gardent pendant quelques générations dans un coin de leur coeur le rêve des vieux ghettos. Grâce à leurs fortunes, aux liens qu'ils conservent entre eux, à l'action qu'ils exercent sur des Gouvernants ignorants, ils représentent une valeur internationale. Ils ne sont et ne peuvent pas être un facteur. Une politique sage doit donc laisser entrevoir aux Juifs une possibilité de groupement en Palestine mais dans les cadres des nationalités existantes et non comme nationalité indépendante." Gout to Margerie, 7 May 1917. Archives Diplomatiques, Ministère des Relations Extérieures, Paris; Guerre 1914–1918, Sionisme III and IV, vol. 1199, folio 7. Cited in David Vital, *Zionism: The Crucial Phase* (Oxford, 1987), p. 196.

2. *The Collected Writings of John Maynard Keynes*, vol. 10 (London, 1972), pp. 10–11.

3. See Hans J. Eysenck, *The Psychology of Politics* (London, 1954); and idem, "Social and Political Attitudes," in *Personality, Genetics, and Behavior* (New York, 1982), pp. 31–35.
4. J. L. Talmon, "Is Force Indeed an Answer to Everything?" *Dispersion and Unity* (Jerusalem) 17–18 (1973): 7–42.
5. *Israel and American Jewish Interaction: Report of an International Task Force* (New York, 1978), pp. 10–12. It is only right to add that I was a member of the task force in question, but, when the draft of its report was shown to me, I became a dissenting member. I did not contest the argument that Israel was central in Jewish life. I did reject what I judged to be the less than clear and forceful terms in which both the diagnostic and the prescriptive parts of the report were couched. And I objected to the American Jewish Committee's management of the drafting of the final report, in the following terms:

> Although attention was evidently paid to the views of the Israeli members of the group, the report strikes me as an entirely Jewish-American document: in style, in approach, and in specific content. Concepts, terminology, points of departure, choice of topics, and conclusions all bear the characteristic stamp of American Jewish public life and affairs. The many (and often all too generous) references to matters on this [i.e., the Israeli] side of the water, to our concerns, our society, our government, and our voluntary public institutions, all seem to have been passed through Jewish-American filters. Much has been dimmed and softened and much has been rendered unreal. While I can understand American Jewish inhibitions on this score, the result, I believe, is that a singular opportunity to get nearer to the heart of the matter has been missed.

I should say that the editors of the report had pressed me very hard to give them a *written* dissenting opinion for publication and that, when it was delivered, they duly and honorably included it among the appendixes to their printed report (pp. 75–78).

153

6. "Note by the Secretary of the War Cabinet," 17 October 1917 (Public Record Office, CAB 21/58), Appendix I(8).
7. Israeli Ministry for Foreign Affairs, *Documents Relating to the Agreement between the Government of Israel and the Government of the Federal Republic of Germany* (Jerusalem, 1953), doc. 1, pp. 10–11.
8. "Note to the Four Occupying Powers," 12 March 1951, ibid., pp. 22–23.
9. 26 October 1951, ibid., doc. 15, pp. 46–47. Emphasis added.

3. Politics, Divergence, and Historical Discontinuity

1. A. J. Toynbee, *A Study of History*, vol. 3 (London, 1934), p. 49.
2. "Ves' vopros," wrote Lenin, "kto kovo operedit?" (17 October 1921). V. I. Lenin, *Polnoe Sobranie Sochinenii* [complete works], 5th ed., vol. 44 (Moscow, 1964), p. 161. I am greatly indebted to my colleague John Bushnell for helping me trace a published source for this famous remark.
3. Gordon Craig, *Germany, 1866–1945* (Oxford, 1978).
4. Lord Robert Cecil, commenting on a dispatch from the High Commissioner in Cairo to the Foreign Secretary, 11 February 1916. Public Record Office, FO 371/2671.
5. Benedetto Croce, *Theory and History of Historiography* [Teoria e storia della storiografia], trans. Douglas Ainslie (London, 1921), esp. pp. 11–26.
6. R. G. Collingwood, *The Idea of History* (Oxford, 1946; rpt. 1973), esp. pp. 231–249.

4. The Matter of Loyalties

1. *Le Monde* (Paris), 23 March 1984.
2. Interview with Mike Wallace on CBS's "Sixty Minutes," 23 October 1988.

154

3. Heinrich Graetz, *History of the Jews,* vol. 5 (Philadelphia, 1962), pp. 3–4.
4. Raymond Aron, *Mémoires* (Paris, 1983), p. 376.
5. *Tikkun* 4 (March-April 1989): 48.
6. *The Times* [London], 4 July 1983. Gerald Kaufman, the MP in question, has since become "shadow" Foreign Secretary on the Labour front bench.
7. Albert Vorspan, "Soul-Searching," *New York Times Magazine,* 8 May 1988.
8. Larry Gross, Frank Furstenberg, et al., *New York Review of Books,* 17 March 1988.

5. The Bifurcation of Jewry

1. In June 1989 the Israeli State Comptroller, Judge Miriam Ben-Porath, published a list of major individual contributors to the parties that had offered candidates in the general election the previous year. Heading the list was Charles Bronfman of Canada, whose contribution to the Labor Party amounted to 2,101,760 New Israeli Shekels (approximately $1,050,000, in 1989 U.S. dollars). A lesser contributor, bearing a somewhat better-known name, was Baron Edmond de Rothschild. His contribution to the Labor Party was given as NIS 320,200 (approximately $160,000). Other parties, including Yitzhak Shamir's Likud, had their share of Diaspora supporters, although none so strikingly as Shimon Peres's Labor Party. On the question whether such contributions are legal, opinion seems to be divided. It is likely that strictly speaking they are not. They are certainly a source of disquiet, however, and steps are being taken to deal with the questions they raise.
2. "Le Juif naît Juif par le fait que ses parents l'étaient mais choisit librement de le rester ou non. Cette liberté diffère-t-elle en nature de celle du Français catholique ou protestant? Réponse malaisée. Au moins dans nos sociétés sécularisées, l'État se veut séparé de

155

toutes les Églises. Le prêtre réduit à l'état laïc, qui jette sa soutane aux orties, devient un citoyen comme les autres, non sans subir parfois la mise en quarantaine par les membres de la communauté qu'il a quittée. En ce qui concerne la nationalité, le Français peut l'échanger contre notre en émigrant vers un pays qui lui accordera, plus ou moins facilement, la citoyenneté. Le Juif déjudaïsé, qui rejette tous les liens avec les autres Juifs, ne renie aucune partie de lui-même; il ne rejette ni sa langue, ni sa morale, ni son mode de vie, puisque tout cela lui vient de ce que l'on appelle son milieu, le pays dans lequel il vit et l'État auquel il obéit. Mais il reste Juif aux yeux des autres." Raymond Aron, *Mémoires* (Paris, 1983), p. 502.

3. One might argue, however, that it was available in eastern Europe (notably in Poland) before the Second World War.

6. State and Nation

1. An example is the following statement by a senior Foreign Office official with special responsibility for Middle Eastern affairs, a statement recorded in his diary at a time when relations between the United Kingdom and Israel were particularly tense. The British were then making what was to be their last serious attempt to restore an order of their own devising to the region. Their plan would have involved a drastic diminution of Israel's territorial, economic, and strategic viability. "I lectured to the Imperial Defence College this morning on the Palestine question," he noted. "Had written it all very carefully this time and it went quite well. I found it cleared my own ideas on the subject, and am left with the strong conviction that the Jews are doomed if they don't change their ways. But they show no signs of recognizing that." Evelyn Shuckburgh, *Descent to Suez: Diaries, 1951–1956* (London, 1986), p. 259.

Index

cism of, 46, 91–100; establishment of, 51, 70, 140; lobbies for, 54–55, 62, 88; and France, 55; and peace process, 95; policy on occupied territories, 95–96, 122; scholarship in, 110; and problem of church and state, 113–115, 117; public debate within, 121; support for political parties in, 155n1. *See also* Zionism

Israel Defense Forces (IDF), 97
Italy, 106

James, William, 37
Jewish Agency for Palestine, 51, 52, 81
Jews: admission of, to civil society, 1, 14–18, 19, 128; hostility to, 3, 8, 18, 24, 33, 98; isolation of, 5–6, 11–12, 23, 24; identity of, 5–6, 109; occupations of, 7–8; privileged vs. underprivileged, 13; and intermarriage, 16, 105, 109; and national question, 23, 25, 48, 77–78, 113, 124, 129, 146; autonomy of, 24, 27, 45; Eastern European, 25–27, 29, 30, 73–74, 132, 139; assimilation of, 27, 109, 138, 147; world outlook of, 28; destruction of, 29, 50, 52, 74, 120, 132, 147; American, 29, 55, 62, 87, 93, 94, 96, 103–104, 108–113, 153n5; transformation of, 29–63; millenary aspirations of, 31–32; and military, 31, 37, 44; myth of international power of, 32, 71; in international politics,

35–44; unity of, 39–40, 72, 119–120, 143–144, 147–148; collective behavior of, 39, 84, 127, 128; communities of, 39, 104–105, 108, 115, 116, 122, 147; bifurcation of, 40, 42–43, 101–117, 131–132, 141–144; divisions among, 42–46, 117, 119, 131, 144; loyalties of, 43, 45, 46, 87–100, 119; culture of, 43, 73, 104, 105, 107, 109, 111, 114, 116, 120, 128, 132, 142, 145, 146; history of, 66–69, 75–85, 124, 129, 146; exile (*galut*) of, 66, 72, 80, 81, 82, 84, 115, 120, 123, 127; impact of modernism on, 73; quietism of, 73, 84; decline of European, 103–108, 109–111, 132; defensiveness of, 105–106; language of, 105, 109, 111, 114, 116, 142, 143; decline of identifiable American, 109–111; scholarship of, 110; anxiety of, 134; survival of, 146–148. *See also* Israel; Zionism

Johnson, Lyndon, 88
Jordan, 60
Josephus, Flavius, 64
Judaism, 1, 15–16, 73, 84, 110–111, 125, 145; divisions within, 43–48; Reform, 45; and national life, 120, 126, 128, 139, 140. *See also* Jews

Kennedy, John F., 88
Keynes, Lord, 35
Klein, Théo, 87–88
Knesset, 122